Christianity is NOT

Religion

James A. Fowler

C.I.Y. Publishing
P.O. Box 1822
Fallbrook, California 92088
http://www.christinyou.net

CHRISTIANITY IS *NOT* RELIGION

Published by C.I.Y. Publishing
P.O. Box 1822
Fallbrook, California 92088-1822

Printed in the United States of America

ISBN – 978-1-929541-24-9

The chapters of this volume were previously published as separate booklets over a period of approximately fifteen (15) years. Though copyrighted individually in that form, they are now copyrighted together in this book.

Table of Contents

FOREWORD

The term "Christianity" is used throughout this volume with a positive connotation. As employed in this book, "Christianity" refers to the eternal, on-going reality of the life and work of the living Lord Jesus, who by the Spirit provides the dynamic of divine presence and function within receptive Christian individuals and communities. As stated in the following chapters, "Christianity is 'Christ-in-you-ity' ... the personal, spiritual presence of the risen and living Lord Jesus, manifesting His life and character in Christians, i.e. 'Christ-ones'" (cf. chapter 1). "Christianity is indicative of everything that Jesus Christ came to *be* and *do*. The entirety of the revelation of God to man is constituted and comprised in the person and work of Jesus Christ" (cf. chapter 10).

One has to admit, however, that reference to "Christianity" has a negative connotation in ever increasing contexts in our modern world.

In many areas of the world the designation "Christianity" conveys the connotation of a Western (primarily European and North American) religion that is inextricably connected with Western civilization and an abundance of cultural accretions. The liberalized moral decadence of Western civilizations – viewed by many in other cultures as "Christian civilization" – has, in fact, fueled a backlash of repudiation against "Christianity" by other religio-cultural societies. Reverting to a radical conservatism of their own religio-cultural values, some have regarded Western religious "Christianity" as the "Great Satan" that threatens their established way of life and religious worship. Islamic fundamentalism and its proclaimed *jihad* against Western thought and religion is the foremost contemporary example of this phenomenon.

In addition to the religio-cultural understanding of the term "Christianity," one has to add the semantic problem of how the word is translated in other languages. French sociologist, Jacques Ellul, notes, for example, in his book, *The Subversion of Christianity* (English title), that the French word for "Christianity" is *christianisme* (original French title of his book, *La Subversion du Christianisme*). In his denial that the reality of Christ is an ...ism (cf. chapter 7 of this book), and without an adequate French word to explain "Christianity" in a positive way, Ellul reverts to utilizing a symbolic "**X**" (interestingly utilized throughout Christian history as a symbol of the cross) to refer to the divine dynamic of the Christ-life in individuals and communities. Various languages employ different words with a wide range of meanings and connotations to refer to the phenomenon of "Christianity."

Even within Western, North American vocabulary the heretofore predominantly positive connotation of the term "Christianity" is rapidly eroding. While teaching at a Christian men's retreat in the Los Angeles, California area, the participants strenuously objected to and denied the assertions that "Christianity is NOT religion," and conversely that "Christianity IS Christ." In their vocabulary the word "Christianity" was synonymously equated with the phenomena of "Christendom" and the "Christian religion" as it is variously expressed in the institutional systems of ecclesiastical churches. Understood in this way "Christianity" is indeed religion, and not necessarily to be identified or equated with the dynamic of the living Christ. Their solution was to refer to the reality of the life and work of the living Lord Jesus simply as "Christ." Who can argue with the choice of His name for all that He is and does?

In light of the continuing erosion of the positive connotation of the term "Christianity," the author seriously questioned whether the articles in this volume should even be published. Perhaps it should be entirely rewritten to avoid the word "Christianity" altogether. But others who have read the articles have encouraged publication, believing that the term "Christianity" and the import of the material in these chapters will be understood by a majority of the intended readership of North American Christians (at least for the present time). Admittedly, a few decades from now this book may be an anachronistic anomaly when the term "Christianity" by the process of language evolution no longer has any positive connotations. By that time genuine Christians who wish to share the reality of the living Lord Jesus will have to find a word that conveys the meaning of what – better Who – they are referring to. Perhaps that designation will simply be "Christ Jesus," as the brethren in Los Angles preferred to refer to the reality that is always singularly HIM.

In a final word it should be noted that these chapters were first prepared as separate studies over a period of several years. Their assembly together in the format of this book does not flow as smoothly as if they were written sequentially for a single treatise. Not only are there numerous redundancies, but the writing style varies from popular to technical, and the length from brief to protracted. These facts aside, there remains in these collected studies a consistent theme, expressed first in negation and finally in affirmation, concerning the essence of the Christian gospel in Jesus Christ alone. It is the author's sincere desire that readers will "focus upon Jesus, the Author and Finisher of faith" (Heb. 12:2).

James A. Fowler
January, 2008

Chapter One

CHRISTIANITY IS *NOT* RELIGION

The need of the hour is to distinguish and differentiate between "religion" and Christianity. Most people in the Western world have so long identified these terms and thought them to be synonymous and equivalent, that it takes a sharp can-opener of rational argument, or the sharper still "Word of God" (Heb. 4:12), to reveal the contrasting dichotomy between Christianity and "religion." This attempt to differentiate between the two may indeed be presumptuous, but on the other hand it might be used of God to bring the revelation of spiritual understanding that would allow someone to make the important distinction and enjoy the reality of Jesus' life.

Many erstwhile Christian thinkers have made the distinction between "religion" and Christianity. Martin

1

Luther, in confronting the sixteenth century religionism of Roman Catholicism, explained, "I have often said that to speak and judge rightly in this matter we must carefully distinguish between a pious (religious) man and a Christian."[1] The Danish philosopher, Soren Kierkegaard, was exposing the nineteenth century religionism of the state church in Denmark in his work entitled *Attack on Christendom*, wherein he noted that it is most difficult to explain to someone who thinks that they are a Christian already, what it means to be a Christian.[2] German theologian, Dietrich Bonhoeffer, stood up to the spineless religionism of the German Lutheran Church during World War II and was killed by the Nazis. In his *Letters and Papers from Prison* he sets up the antinomy between faith and religion and argues for a "nonreligious" or "religionless Christianity."[3]

Perhaps the clearest delineation between "religion" and Christianity is drawn by the Swiss theologian, Karl Barth, arguably the greatest theologian of the twentieth century. In his voluminous *Church Dogmatics*, Barth wrote that

"the revelation of God is the abolition of religion."[4]

2

"It is always the sign of definite misunderstanding when an attempt is made to systematically coordinate revelation and religion...to fix their mutual relationship."[5]

"In opposition to all 'religionism' the proclamation of the grace of God is introduced as the truth..."[6]

"Religion is unbelief. It is a concern of...godless man."[7]

"Religion is clearly seen to be a human attempt to anticipate what God in His revelation wills to do and does do. It is the attempted replacement of the divine work by a human manufacture."[8]

"It is a feeble but defiant, an arrogant but hopeless, attempt to create something which man could do. In religion man bolts and bars himself against revelation by providing a substitute, by taking away in advance the very thing which has to be given by God. It is never the truth. It is a complete fiction, which has not only little but no relation to God."[9]

"What is the purpose of the universal attempt of religions but to anticipate God, to foist a human product into the place of His word, to make our own images of the One who is known only where He gives Himself to be known."[10]

"The revelation of God denies that any religion is true. No religion can stand before the grace of God as true religion."[11]

French sociologist and legal scholar, Jacques Ellul, in like manner affirms that,

"There is no path leading from a little bit of religion (of whatever kind) to a little more and finally to faith. Faith shatters all religion..."[12]

"The opposition between religion and revelation can really be understood quite simply. We can reduce it to a maxim: religion goes up, revelation comes down.[13]

3

"The central fact of the revelation of the God of Abraham, Isaac and Jacob, the God of Jesus Christ, is that God descends to humankind. Never in any way, under any circumstances can we ascend to God, howsoever slightly."[14]

The American Episcopalian priest, Robert Capon, has an inimical straightforward way of explaining the difference between religion and Christianity.

"Almost all people, inside as well as outside the church, find that the notion of grace stands in contradiction to everything they understand by religion."[15]

"The gospel of grace is the end of religion, the final posting of the CLOSED sign on the sweatshop of the human race's perpetual struggle to think well of itself. For that, at bottom, is what religion is: man's well-meant but dim-witted attempt to approve of his unapprovable condition by doing odd jobs he thinks some important Something will thank him for.

"Religion, therefore, is a loser, a strictly fallen activity. It has a failed past and a bankrupt future. There was no religion in Eden and there won't be any in heaven; and in the meantime Jesus has died and risen to persuade us to knock it all off right now."[16]

"I want you to set aside the notion of the Christian religion, because it's a contradiction in terms. You won't learn anything positive about religion from Christianity, and if you look for Christianity in religion, you'll never find it. To be sure, Christianity uses the forms of religion, and, to be dismally honest, too many of its adherents act as if it were a religion; but it isn't one, and that's that. The church is not in the religion business; it is in the Gospel-proclaiming business. And the gospel is the good news that all man's fuss and feathers over his relationship with God is unnecessary because God, in the mystery of the Word who is Jesus, has gone and fixed it up Himself. So let that pass."[17]

4

Many other statements from Christian writers could be adduced, but these will suffice to represent the awareness of the differentiation between "religion" and Christianity.

Background of the word "religion"

A brief study of the etymology of our English word "religion" will reveal that we might not want to allow the word "religion" to be associated with Christianity. There are several Latin words that may have served as the origin of our English word "religion." The Latin word *religo* meant "to tie or fasten."[18] A similar word, *religio*, was used to refer to "respect, devotion or superstition." *Religio* was a recognition that men are often tied or bound to God in reverence or devotion. It can also convey the meaning of being bound or tied to a set of rules and regulations, to rituals of devotion, to a creedal belief-system, or to a cause, ideology, or routine. Some have suggested that "religion" may be derived from the Latin word *relegere*, which refers to re-reading. There is no doubt that "religion" is often associated with repetitious rites of liturgy and litany, and the reproduction of creedal formulas and expressions. Most etymologists, however, regard the English word "religion" to be derived from the Latin word *religare* which is closely aligned with the root word *religo*.[19] The prefix *re-* means "back" or "again," and the word *ligare* refers to "binding, tying or attaching." Other English words such as "ligature," referring to "something that is used to bind," and "ligament" which "binds things together," evidence the same root in the Latin word *ligare*. The Latin word *religare*, from which our English word "religion" is most likely derived, meant "to tie back" or "to bind up."

The purpose of Jesus' coming was not to "bind us" or "tie us" to anything or anyone, though it might be argued that in the reception of Jesus Christ by faith there is a spiritual attachment of our identity with Him. Jesus clearly indicates that He came to set us free – free to be functional humanity in the fullest sense, by allowing God to function through us to His glory. To some believing Jews, Jesus explained that "you shall know the truth, and the truth shall make you free" (John 8:32). Further explanation of the personification of that "truth" in Himself was then made when Jesus said, "If therefore the Son shall make you free, you shall be free indeed." To the Galatians Paul affirms that, "It was for freedom that Christ set us free; therefore do not be subject again to a yoke of slavery" by reverting back to the bondage of Jewish religion (Gal. 5:1). "You were called to freedom, brethren" (Gal. 5:13), Paul exclaims. "Where the spirit of the Lord is, there is liberty" (II Cor. 3:17).

Jesus did not say, "I came that you might have religion, and practice it more faithfully," or "I came that you might have religion, and adhere to it more committedly," or "I came that you might have religion, and define it more dogmatically," or "I came that you might have religion, and defend it more vehemently," or "I came that you might have religion, and thus behave more morally." What Jesus said was, "I came that you might have life, and have it more abundantly" (John 10:10). The life that He came to bring and express within us and through us is His life. "I AM the way, the truth and the life," declared Jesus to His disciples (John 14:6). The apostle John wrote that "He that has the Son has life; he that does not have the Son does not have life" (I John 5:12). "Christ is our life," is the phrase Paul uses in writing to the Colossians (Col. 3:4), for Christianity is not "religion," but the life of Jesus Christ expressed in receptive humanity.

Biblical usage of the word "religion"

A closer look at the biblical usage of the word "religion" will demonstrate that the word is seldom used with any positive implication, but generally has a negative connotation.

When Paul traveled to Athens he observed an abundance of idols, even an idol to an "unknown god," lest they might have missed any. Paul stands up and declares, "Men of Athens, I observe that you are very religious in all respects" (Acts 17:22). What does Paul mean by referring to their pervasive idolatry as being "religious?" The Greek word that Paul used was *deisidaimon*, which is derived from two other Greek words: *deido*, meaning "to fear or respect," and *daimon*, the word for "demon." What Paul was saying was that he had observed that they had "great fear or respect for demons," and were thus very religious or superstitious. Festus used the same Greek word to pejoratively refer to the Jewish religion, when he explained to King Agrippa that the Jews who brought charges against Paul "had some points of disagreement with him about their own religion" (Acts 25:19).

In his epistle to the Colossians, Paul was confronting the regional religionism of Asia as well as the Judaizing

8

religionism that constantly followed his ministry. He wanted to show the superiority of the gospel of grace in Jesus Christ over all religion. In referring to the moralistic activities that religionists were attempting to impose upon the Christian believers in Colossae, Paul asks, "Why do you submit yourself to decrees, such as 'Do not handle, do not taste, do not touch!'? These are matters which have the appearance of wisdom in self-made religion and self-abasement and severe treatment of the body, but are of no value against fleshly indulgence" (Col. 2:20-23). The word translated "religion" is the Greek word *ethelothreskia*, which is a combination of two other Greek words: *ethelo* meaning "will, desire, delight or pleasure," and *threskeia* meaning "worship or religion." Paul is describing such moralistic religious actions as "will-worship" of "self-made religion"; activities which man imposes upon himself and others, believing that such willed self-effort serves as a benefit before God in moralistic performance. Paul denies the veracity of such thinking, regarding such as mere "self-made religion," and of no benefit against the selfish patterns of fleshly indulgence.

James explains that, "If anyone thinks himself to be religious, and yet does not bridle his tongue but deceives his own heart, this man's religion is worthless" (James 1:26,27). The Greek word that he uses is *threskeia*, meaning "worship or religion." Misrepresentation of the character of God in our behavior often indicates that we are engaging in "worthless religion." James continues, though, to use *threskeia* in a positive way when he refers to "pure and undefiled religion" (James 1:27), wherein the worth-ship of God's character is genuinely expressed in practical ministry to orphans and widows, and in the expression of the purity of God's character. In that case genuine Christian worship transpires as we are receptive to the activity of God and express the worth-ship of His character in our behavior.

In light of the predominantly negative inferences of the word "religion" in the New Testament, we should avoid applying this word to Christianity.

Christianity and "world religions"

Failure to differentiate between Christianity and "religion" has caused many to lump Christianity together as just another "religion" in the study of comparative world religions. Their criteria for the consideration of a "religion" is merely sociological, psychological, creedal, liturgical or

10

organizational, all of which are inadequate to consider the radical uniqueness of Christianity.

The story is told of Gautama Buddha, who lived some four hundred years prior to the birth of Jesus Christ. He was dying. Some of his devotees came to Buddha and asked how they should perpetuate his memory. "How should we share with the world the remembrance of you? How shall we memorialize you?" Buddha responded, "Don't bother! It is not me that matters; it is my teaching that should be propagated and adhered to throughout the world."

Does that seem to be self-effacing? Does that sound like a noble ideal that attempts to avoid egocentricity? "Don't focus on me, just remember my teaching."

If Jesus had said something like that, it would certainly legitimize much of what we observe all around us today in the so-called "Christian religion." The "Christian religion" that has formed around the teaching of Christianity is involved in the propagation of various understandings of Jesus' teaching as determined by various interpretations of the Bible. Most of those who call themselves "Christians" today seem to think that Jesus advocated the same thing that Buddha is alleged to have uttered. "Don't focus on me, just remember my teaching."

11

Jesus did not say anything like that! In fact, what Buddha said is contrary to everything Jesus taught, and everything recorded in the New Testament scriptures. Jesus did not say, "Just remember my teaching." Jesus said, "I AM the resurrection and the life" (John 11:25). "I AM the way, the truth and the life" (John 14:6). He did not say, "I will show you the way; I will teach you the truth; I will give you the life." His own indwelling presence is the only way for man to be man as God intended. The reality of His person is the truth of God. The very personal presence of the risen Lord Jesus is the life of the Living God, the ontological essence of everything He came to bring to this world. In Buddhism the person of Buddha may not be of any importance except for historical observation, but in Christianity the risen and living Person of Jesus Christ is the reality of God's presence restored to mankind.

Another story is told of Sadhu Sundar Singh[20], a convert from the religion of Sikhism to Christianity, who eventually became one of India's most well-known Christians. A European professor of comparative religions (who was himself an agnostic) interviewed the former Sadhu one day, with the evident intention of showing him

12

his mistake in renouncing another religion for what he perceived to be the "Christian religion."

The professor asked Mr. Singh, "What have you found in the Christian religion that you did not have in your old religion?" Sundar Singh answered, "I have Jesus." "Yes, I know," the professor replied somewhat impatiently, "but what particular principles or doctrines have you found that you did not have before?" Sunday Singh replied, "The particular person I have found is Jesus."

Try as he might, the professor could not budge him from that position. He went away discomfited but thoughtful.

Sundar Singh was right. The religions of the world have some fine teachings, but they lack the person and life of Jesus Christ, the dynamic presence of God in man.

A personal friend, Bill Hekman, was once seated on an airplane and struck up a conversation with the gentleman seated next to him. In their conversation the fellow-passenger explained that he was a Professor of Islamic Studies. Bill Hekman indicated that he was a Christian and had been a missionary to Irian Jaya for twenty years, and that he was returning to Indonesia to engage in Christian teaching.

Their conversation eventually included a discussion of the extent to which the peoples of Indonesia had converted from the predominant religion of Islam to Christianity, and a mutual questioning of whether the Indonesian government statistics of the percentages of Muslims and Christians were accurate. Then the professor of Islamic studies said something very surprising. He indicated that he thought that Indonesia would someday be a primarily Christian nation. Bill, though obviously hopeful of such, was taken aback by such a prediction, and asked him why he thought that this would take place. The professor replied, "Because the Christians have *Roh Allah*." *Roh Allah* is the Indonesian expression for the "Spirit of God." This professor realized that there was a dynamic and power in the "Spirit of God" that was beyond anything that Islam had in their belief-system that traced back to the teaching of Mohammed. Indeed there is, for the "Spirit of Christ" is the vital dynamic of the living Lord Jesus, who as God comes to live in the Christian and empower him for the out-working of God's character and work. May his surprising prediction prove true!

There are many religions in the world, such as Buddhism, Hinduism, Taoism, Confucianism,

Mohammedanism (Islam), and Judaism. The ideologies of humanism and communism have also been identified as religions, as well as the individualism of "The American religion."[21] The tenets of Christianity can also be incorporated into a religion of "Christianism,"[22] or the "Christian religion" as we are referring to this phenomenon within this study.

Christianity cannot legitimately be compared to any of these religions, however. Religion and Christianity are as different as night and day, death and life, fiction and truth. To attempt to include Christianity in a course on "comparative world religions" is to compare that which cannot be compared, like comparing apples with oranges. Christianity is unique. It is one of a kind. It is the singular reality of God's activity to restore mankind from their fallen condition through His Son, Jesus Christ. Christianity is not the propagation of a philosophy. It is not the performance of religious procedures. It is not the perpetuation of an organizational program. Christianity is the reception of a Person, Jesus Christ, the Son of God, God Himself, into one's being and behavior.

In all of the world's religions, you can take away the founder and still have the religion. You can take Buddha out of Buddhism and still have the Four Noble Truths and the Eight-fold Path. You can take Mohammed out of Islam, and still have the Five Pillars of Action and the Six Articles of Belief. And yes, tragically, you can take Christ out of that misnomer of "Christian religion," and still have the doctrines and the programs and the organizational machinery that masquerade as the "church." Liberal theologians within the "Christian religion" have indicated that it does not matter whether there was ever an "historical Jesus," as long as the "religion" benefits a person psychologically and ethically. On such a premise of subjective religious impact being the existential essence of the "Christian religion," they go about "demythologizing" the New Testament scriptures to reduce them to psychological and ethical tenets.

The hypothetical question might be asked, "If God could and would die tonight, what would happen to the 'Christian religion' tomorrow?" The answer is "Nothing!" The "Christian religion" would keep right on functioning, because Jesus Christ, as God, is not the essence and the dynamic of what they are doing anyway! If God were to die tonight, it would be "business as usual" for religion

16

tomorrow. It does not require God in Christ for the "Christian religion" to function; just man and money!

Genuine Christianity, on the other hand, requires the presence and function of the life and person of the living Lord Jesus. Christianity is Christ! Jesus Christ is not just the historical founder of a "Christian religion"; rather He is the vital spiritual essence of Christianity that is His dynamic ontological function within receptive humanity.

Another hypothetical question might be asked: "If you could take Christ out of Christianity, what would be left?" Again it is possible to answer, "Nothing!" Or it is possible that we might explain that the resultant spiritual vacuum is what we know as the "Christian religion." It has been suggested that if you take Christ out of Christianity, all you have left is the self-oriented, self-perpetuating religion of "-I-anity," which is an inanity.

South African author, Albert Nolan, explains that

"Jesus cannot be fully identified with that great religious phenomenon of the Western world known as Christianity (Christian religion). He was much more than the founder of one of the world's great religions. He stands above Christianity (Christian religion) as the judge of all it has done in His name."[23] (parentheses added)

The "Christian religion" is a misnomer. Christianity is not religion! It is so radically different from all religion that it cannot properly be compared with the "world religions." All attempts to do so have preemptively reduced Christianity into its bastardized counterfeit of "Christian religion."

Scripture interpretation and "religion"

The new covenant implemented in the Person and work of Jesus Christ was designed to supplant and supersede all of the old forms of religion that had existed since the fall of man. Careful study of the new covenant literature, which we know as the New Testament, evidences the constant exposure of the radical difference between religion and the dynamic life of Jesus Christ in the kingdom of grace.

Beginning in the accounts of the life and ministry of Jesus in the Gospels, it is apparent that Jesus was constantly confronting religion[24] as He proclaimed the kingdom of grace that He came to reveal in Himself. The Pharisees and scribes of Judaism were the religionists who placed themselves in antagonism to all that Jesus did and said. They did not have the spiritual understanding to comprehend what Jesus was proclaiming. Approximately one-third of Jesus' teaching was in parables, which only served to befuddle the religious teachers for they seldom realized that Jesus was comparing their religious *modus operandi* with the function of the spiritual reign of God that He came to bring in Himself. Eventually the religious leaders realized that the parables were exposing them, and they began to take measures to silence their nemesis by execution.

In the Acts of the Apostles, Luke carefully explains that in the earliest history of the church, the initial Christian leaders were progressively made aware of the radical difference between the Christian gospel and all religion. Christianity had to be unencumbered and unhindered from any identification with Judaic religion. Peter's dream in Joppa, the inclusion of Cornelius and the Gentiles, the antagonism of the Jewish leaders in Judea, all represent pictorial vignettes of the progressive awareness of how Christianity had to break free from all religion.

Paul's epistles bear the repetitive theme of explaining the difference between religion and Christianity. In his epistle to the Romans, Paul explains that righteousness is not in religious rites or the Law, but in Jesus Christ, the Righteous One. In the epistle we know as First Corinthians, Paul counters the religious excesses that were developing in the young church at Corinth. In the epistle we identify as

19

Second Corinthians, Paul carefully differentiates between gospel ministry by the grace of God and the manipulations of religious method being evidenced by the intrusive pretenders. Writing to the Galatians, Paul pits the gospel versus religion, forcefully denying that there is "another gospel" as inculcated by legalistic religion. In contrast to religious exclusivism, Paul explains to the Ephesians that all men become a new humanity in Jesus Christ. Combating the effects of the regional religionism of Asia, Paul wrote to the Colossians emphasizing the pre-eminence of Jesus Christ, who is our life. In all of Paul's epistles the theme of Christianity as distinct from and confronting religion is to be found.

The writer of the epistle to the Hebrews likewise explains how the old and new covenants of God are to be differentiated, and the old tenets of Judaic religion are replaced by the life of Jesus Christ. The epistle of James indicates that merely going through the rituals of religion is vain, but Christian faith is the outworking of the life of Jesus Christ.

The Revelation of Christ as witnessed by John is indeed the climax of the new covenant literature. In pictorial form Jesus reveals that religion will continually attempt to overcome and secularize Christianity as it was doing in the seven churches of Asia. Jesus is the victor over religion[25], though, and will overcome all the onslaughts of conflict that will inevitably come between Christianity and religion.

Throughout the entirety of the New Testament there is a continuous explanation of the difference between Christianity and religion. Why has this not been made more apparent to Christians in order that they might be more discerning and cease to equate the two? Dare we explain that the interpretation of the new covenant scriptures has been done primarily by commentators and theologians who are thoroughly inundated in "Christian religion?" Religious interpreters whose very livelihood is on the line would be hesitant to expose their own religious methods, even if they had the spiritual discernment to recognize that such religious practices were being exposed in the scriptures. We have witnessed a tragic history of misinterpretation of the Bible throughout the history of "Christian religion."

Evangelism and "religion"

The history of such misinterpretation also serves to explain why the gospel has been received so slowly throughout the world in the last two thousand years.

"Christian religion" could only offer their brand of religion that "tied" people to a belief-system and "bound" them to moralistic rules and regulations in "attachment" to the ecclesiastical institution.

Jesus and the early church, on the other hand, proclaimed the gospel by contrasting the grace of God in Jesus Christ with the premises and methodology of religion. They exposed the self-serving practices of religion by manifesting and explaining God's desire to restore all men in Jesus Christ. They confronted the selfish inequities of religion with the love of God in Christ.

Does it not seem self-evident that the ineffectual efforts of evangelism engaged in by "Christian religion" through these many centuries are a result of proclaiming a belief-system to be assented to and advocating a morality to be adhered to, rather than offering the life of Jesus Christ to be received by faith? "Christian religion" usurped the message of Christianity, complete with all the abominable methods that are indicative of all religion, which are antithetical to God's functional intent in Jesus Christ.

"Christian religion" has become so thoroughly religionized that it is unable to perceive the contrast between Christianity and religion. They engage in the religious methodology of recruitment by propaganda in order to "bind, tie and attach" increasing numbers of people to the propositional ideology, the activistic cause, and the sociological organization they represent. Their contemporary marketing procedures of "church growth" reveal that they know nothing of the experience of the dynamic of the grace of God expressed in the living Lord Jesus by His Spirit.

Genuine evangelism is witnessing to the "good news" of the life of Jesus Christ as He comes to indwell us by His Spirit and live out the divine character in our behavior in contrast to the performance of religion. When an individual can see the impotence of religion, having experienced the frustration of religious performance, then the grace of God in Jesus Christ will be "good news" indeed. Such was Paul's testimony in Philippians 3:2-14 when he identified religion as a "total loss" and "nothing but rubbish," but rejoiced in his personal and spiritual identification with the living Lord Jesus.

Understanding the difference between Christianity and religion will make all the difference in the world in the way that we engage in evangelism. Rather than presenting unbelievers with a package of doctrine to believe in, or a codification of behavior to conform to, or a sociological institution to join and be involved in, Christians will allow the living Lord Jesus to "re-present" Himself to His created human beings through them, contrasting what He came to bring in Himself with all religious method as He did during His personal and historical incarnational ministry here on earth.

The abuse of humanity in "religion"

In his *Provincial Letters*, Blaise Pascal charges the Jesuits with "sporting with religion, in order to gratify the worst passions of man."[26] It is inherent within the methodology of all man-made religion to offer a counterfeit fulfillment to the needs of mankind. Religion sets itself up in a self-deified position to extend a false-fulfillment of man's God-given desires with a "religious" solution. When the basic God-given needs of man are offered false-fulfillment in religious counterfeit, humanity is being used and abused.

Here are some examples of God-given desires being falsely fulfilled by religion. The God-given desire to be loved is offered a cheap imitation of "a thing called love," wherein one might develop a degree of intimacy with others. The desire to be accepted is appeased as religion offers to accept a person "just as they are," until further instructed. Our human desire to belong is offered false-fulfillment in the encouragement to "get involved" in the "fellowship" of our "community." The desire for sociability is stroked when religion invites a person to relate to their group and let them be their "family." Man's desire for security is offered the secure provision of "once saved, always saved." Religion offers uniformity and conformity to satisfy mans need for order. The basic desire to believe and to be correct in that belief is placated with dogmatism, intellectualism, and the absolutism of orthodoxy. Religion offers a *raison d'etre* and a *cause celebre* to satisfy our need for meaning. Stimulating emotional "highs" and experiential subjectivism provide for the desire for excitement. The need for uniqueness is provided for in the exclusivism and elitism that posits that "we are the only ones." If it is identity that you need, join with us and you will be "somebody," a socialistic identity by association. Religion offers approval and affirmation, often by affirming "I'm OK; you're OK." The desire to work can be accommodated by religious activism that encourages adherents to "get involved" and "work for Jesus." The desire to possess is titillated by the "health and wealth" gospel that falsely asserts that "God wants you rich." The need to give is a favorite target of religion as they urge people to contribute by tithing ten-percent of their income. Religion promises to fulfill the need for destiny by providing the correct techniques, procedures and formulas whereby a person will be guaranteed a place in heaven.

These religious counterfeits are nothing less that an abuse of humanity. Instead of leading mankind out of the addictive false-fulfillment of their God-given desires, religion offers nothing but another form of addictive dysfunction. Religion is co-dependent to the sins of the people. Religion is an aider and abettor to the sinful dysfunction of humanity, enabling and encouraging mankind to seek their solutions and their "salvation" in religion rather than in Jesus Christ.

The satanic source of "religion"

Religion is the devil's playground. The diabolic efforts to inhibit and impede the gospel have been ever so subtle, as they turned Christianity into the "Christian religion," continuing to use the same vocabulary, and using the very inspired scriptures that were designed to be the written record of the revelation of God in Jesus Christ as the basis of their belief-systems and morality codes.

Major W. Ian Thomas writes,

> "It is one of the subtleties of Satan which causes men to flee from God and seek to silence His voice in the very practice of religion. So it is that man, to suit his own convenience, has reduced God to a theological formula, an ethical code, or political program, a theatrical performance in a religious setting, the hero worship of some vivid personality..."[27]

In his masterful presentation of diabolic activity, *The Screwtape Letters*, C.S. Lewis has the senior devil, Screwtape, say to his nephew, Wormwood, "One of our greatest allies at present is the church itself,"[28] i.e. "Christian religion." In another vignette Screwtape explains that "it will be an ill day for us if what most humans mean by 'religion' ever vanishes from the Earth. It can still send us the truly delicious sins. Nowhere do we tempt so successfully as on the very steps of the altar."[29] Blaise Pascal likewise noted that "men never do evil so completely and cheerfully as when they do it from religious conviction."[30]

To identify religion with the activity of Satan will seem to be blasphemous to those who have not differentiated between Christianity and religion. Once that distinction has been clearly made however, the antithetical alternative to

Christianity that takes place in religion will of necessity be identified with the activity of the Evil One.

Norman Olson explains that

> "Satan uses religion and the idea of 'doing good' to make people blind to the fact that these have no saving value whatever, to say nothing of spirituality.
> "Any system of religion is satanic in nature, no matter how beautiful the package might appear to be. Satan is the author of 'do good'."
> "Religion is often portrayed by the devil as a mass solution to man's problem. If he can get everyone into some religion, he knows that he can keep people in some false hope, in some anesthetic, and prevent them from seeing their real need. Nothing that Satan has ever devised has been as successful as religion in blinding men's minds to the truth."[31]

In like manner, Dave Hunt has written that,

> "Satan's primary tactic in opposing God is not to foster atheism, but religion. A perverted 'Christianity' is Satan's ultimate weapon."[32]

If we are to understand religion correctly we must recognize its satanic source and the spiritual conflict that is taking place between God and Satan in Christianity and religion.

The sociological attachment of "religion"

It might be pointed out that mankind has a natural tendency to develop religious practices, and that every known civilization of man has engaged in some form of

28

religion. Indeed it is "natural" for man to form religions, for "the natural man does not understand spiritual things" (I Cor. 2:14). His "natural" wisdom is demonically inspired (James 3:15), for "the prince of the power of the air is the spirit that works in the sons of disobedience" (Eph. 2:2).

Sociologists have on occasion argued that religion serves a beneficial social purpose of attaching people together in group-unity. Such social bonding ties a group of people together as they set their sights on a "higher" common goal. Religion thus gives a group of people a collective sense of identity, purpose and meaning, and provides for social continuity. When engaged in such a collective mutual pursuit of religious striving, their religion provides a legitimacy and validity to the rules and regulations that are imposed upon them, and when religion wanes the weight and authority of social and moral law diminishes.

It is indeed possible to analyze religion sociologically or psychologically$_{33}$, but these are just observations of the phenomena of religion. It cannot be concluded from these observations that religion constitutes a social or moral "good," or that religion is the "better" or "highest" feature of the natural world system of man, especially when it is abusing people as previously noted. Religion is, on the contrary, the most subtle and insidious feature of the diabolically inspired world of natural men, and as such it is the most abominable and damnable.

There is nothing "good" about religion. Religion relativizes the goodness that is derived from God alone. Religion engages in the relativistic goodness of the "good and evil" game that has been played by natural man ever since man fell by partaking of "the tree of the knowledge of good and evil" (Gen. 3).

The world's view of "religion"

Many of those who call themselves "Christians" have been unable to differentiate between Christianity and religion. As they participate in the counterfeit of "Christian religion," they mistakenly think it is Christianity, and are blinded in the belief that religion is an admirable pursuit.

On the other hand, there are many who are not Christians who view the activities of the "Christian religion," and who likewise fail to differentiate between religion and Christianity. They in turn reject Christianity, believing it to be equivalent to the "Christian religion" they have observed.

Many abominable activities have taken place under the guise of "Christian religion." Man-made religion always seeks power and will revert to militaristic warfare to achieve that power. The history of religion, including "Christian religion," is but a succession of religious wars wherein religionists slaughter one another under the flag of "religion," usually with political overtones. The Crusades of the eleventh, twelfth and thirteenth centuries are but one historical example among many.

Religious bigotry has been evident in every century as religious leaders engage in racial, national, sexual, ideological and denominational exclusion, ostracism and persecution. There are always the religious attempts to purge those who disagree, and to punish those who do not conform to legislated morality. The period of the Inquisition is a sad example in the history of "Christian religion."

People of the world observe the big religious organizations with their huge ecclesiastic superstructures. They are often rich, powerful, tax-evading, and political in nature. They observe the religious fanatics who try to justify any activity from bombing an abortion clinic to murdering a doctor who works therein. Any means seems

31

to be justifiable if it achieves their religiously deified end-cause. They observe the seemingly endless and meaningless religious activities of church services, ceremonies and programs that seem to be just "pomp and circumstance."

Is it any wonder that many of the people of the world speak derisively of religion? They have read their history books and have heard of the atrocities perpetrated in the name of "religion." They hear of the vast gold reserves and corporate holdings of religious conglomerates gained through tax-exemptions and unfair advantage. They can see the exploitation of the populace through superstition and fear. They see through the ecclesiastic politicizing and cultural manipulation. They see the people going through their meaningless motions of religious ritual to try to appease God. Often they have come to the conclusion that they do not want anything to do with "religion," and I, for one, do not blame them! The world has a right, even an intellectual obligation, to reject the religious folderol that is so prevalent, and to demand reality.

Was Marx correct in his conclusion that "religion is the opiate of the people"?

Christianity is not "religion"

Religion emphasizes precepts, propositions, performance, production, programs, promotion, percentages, etc. Christianity emphasizes the Person of Jesus Christ, and His life lived out through the receptive Christian believer.

Religion has to do with form, formalism and formulas; ritual, rules, regulations and rites; legalism, laws and laboring. The "good news" of Christianity is that it is not what we do or perform, but what Jesus has done and is doing in us. Jesus exclaimed from the cross, "It is finished!" (John 19:30). The performance is hereby accomplished! Jesus has done all the doing that needs doing for our regeneration, and continues to do all the doing that God wants to do in us. "God is at work in you both to will and to work for His good pleasure" (Phil. 2:13).

Some have tried to explain that "Christianity is not religion; it is a relationship." Such a statement is too ambiguous, for it is possible to have a "relationship" with religious peoples and practices. Although Christianity does involve a personal relationship between an individual and the living Lord Jesus, it must be pointed out that this is effected by the ontological presence of the Spirit of Christ dwelling within the spirit of a Christian who has received Him by faith, and the Spirit of Christ functioning through that Christian's behavior. It is not just a casual relationship of acquaintance with the historical Jesus or with the theological formulations of Jesus' work. Perhaps it would be better to indicate that "Christianity is not religion; it is the reality of Jesus Christ as God coming in the form of His Spirit to indwell man in order to restore him to the functional intent of God whereby the character of God is allowed to be manifested in man's behavior to the glory of God.

Christianity is not religion! Christianity is Christ! Christianity is "Christ-in-you-ity." Jesus Christ did not found a religion to remember and reiterate His teaching. Christianity is the personal, spiritual presence of the risen and living Lord Jesus Christ, manifesting His life and character in Christians, i.e. "Christ-ones." Paul explained, "It is no longer I who live, but Christ lives in me; and the life I now live in the flesh I live by faith in the Son of God, who loved me and gave Himself up for me" (Gal. 2:20).

Chapter Two

CHRISTIANITY IS *NOT* A BOOK RELIGION

Do you know what an iconoclast is?

An iconoclast is an idol-smasher, an idol-breaker. Throughout the history of mankind and religion there have been men and movements that have been iconoclastic. They are always hated by the religionists because religionists do not like to have their "sacred cows" smashed. They worship those idols. In fact, on many occasions in history the religionists have risen up to kill the iconoclasts.

I can almost see the stones. I can almost feel the tar and feathers. I can almost hear the flak and the abusive railings that will be the probable result of my idol-smashing. But iconoclasts believe in what they are doing, and often rush in where angels fear to tread.

I want to be very delicate and selective in my idol-smashing. I know that I am at great risk of being misunderstood and misconstrued. Religionists will hate me for my radical departure from their traditionalism. They will likely misrepresent what I am saying in trumped up charges of treason and by black-listing me for blatant blasphemy.

Can it really be that bad? It could be, but I trust that you will understand what I am saying in this chapter.

With a big backswing I take my first big swipe at the idol by declaring, "Christianity is not a Book-religion." In the previous chapter the assertion was made, "Christianity is not a religion" that binds us to something. The thesis is now amplified by declaring that "Christianity is not a Book-religion." Nor is Christianity the "religion of the Bible" as many have declared.

What is the Bible? The Bible is a book. The word "Bible" is derived from the Greek word *biblion* meaning "book," or more accurately "papyrus scroll," as this was the material used for writing in ancient times. The Bible is a book that is in one sense like every other book in the world, but in another sense is unlike any other book in the world. It is like other books in that it is black printing (sometimes red and other colors) on white paper, and it is a tangible, perishable object. It is unlike other books in that it witnesses to and enscripturates the revelation of God, and is the only book in the world where you have to know the Author to understand the book.

God never intended that we should worship the Book. That is bibliolatry – making the Bible into a physical idol. The reverence that many Christians attach to the book is dangerously close to idolatry of the Bible.

Christianity is not the religion of the Book. Christianity is Christ! Christianity is the dynamic, personal Spirit of God functioning in man. It is not the study of, memorization of, or adherence to the principles and propositions and precepts of a bound-book.

Do you see the distinction I am trying to make? I am attempting to exalt Jesus Christ over the Bible. Frankly, that is a dangerous thing to do these days in contemporary Christian circles, for you begin to smash people's idols.

Unbiblical Understandings of the Bible

Driving through Vista, California, I observed this statement on the marquee of a church building called Calvary Chapel: "The traditions of men cannot save – Trust in the Bible." What kind of salvation can be effected by trusting in the Bible? It is true that "the traditions of men cannot save," but neither can the tradition of "trusting in the Bible." Scripture encourages us to trust in Jesus Christ for salvation for He is our Savior, not the Bible. The personal indwelling life of Jesus Christ alone is effective for salvation. We receive Him (Jesus) by faith, not by "trusting in the Bible."

I received in the mail a tract written by James R. Urban and entitled, "The Bible: Man's Only Hope." The title caused me to suspect that this was misguided hope. The contents only served to confirm such:

> "The Bible is man's only hope for salvation."[1]

Paul indicates that "Christ Jesus...is our hope" (I Timothy 1:1). Luke records Peter's telling the Jewish leaders that "there is salvation in no one else; for there is no other name under heaven that has been given among men, by which we must be saved" (Acts 4:12), other than "the name of Jesus Christ" (Acts 4:10).

> "Abraham Lincoln said, 'I believe the Bible is the best gift that God has ever given to man.'"[2]

The best gift that God has given to man is His Son, Jesus Christ. "God so loved the world that He gave His only begotten Son..." (John 3:16). "The gift of God is eternal life in Christ Jesus our Lord" (Romans 6:23).

> "Horace Greely said, ...The principles of the Bible are the foundation of human freedom.'"[3]

The foundation of human freedom is in Jesus Christ. "It was for freedom that Christ set us free." (Galatians 5:1) "You shall know the truth, and the truth shall make you free" (John 8:32); "I am the...truth" (John 14:6).

> "You will do well to remember this simple formula: 'The best thing to do with the Bible is to know it in your head, stow it in your heart, sow it in the world and show it in your life. For the knowing, stowing, sowing and showing Christian will be a glowing and a growing Christian.'"[4]

A Christian is to "grow in the grace and knowledge of our Lord and Savior Jesus Christ" (II Peter 3:18), not merely by Bible knowledge. The dynamic of the life of Jesus Christ is the basis of our Christian living, not static information of the Bible.

A bestselling book by John MacArthur, Jr. contains what is perhaps the classic defense of bibliolatrous reverence for the Bible. The following quotations are but a few of his assertions:

> "God's Word (the Bible) is true and absolutely comprehensive."[5]

Only God is absolutely comprehensive. The attributes of God are non-transferrable and we cannot attribute an attribute of God to a book. What God is, only God is!

> "its (the Bible's) truthfulness produces a comprehensive righteousness in those who accept it."[6]

The Bible does not produce righteousness. Righteousness is only produced in the behavior of mankind when the Righteous One, Jesus Christ (I John 2:1) dwells in man and the Righteous character of God is expressed in man's behavior as we walk by faith.

> "There is no substitute for submission to Scripture."[7]

James admonishes us to "submit to God" (James 4:7), but we are never admonished to submit to scripture.

> "trust in the inexhaustible sufficiency of our Lord's perfect Word (Bible)."[8]

Our sufficiency is of God (II Corinthians 3:5) from whom we have "all sufficiency in everything" (II Corinthians 9:8). We are to trust in His sufficiency, not that of a book.

> "If we obey it (the Bible), we will be blessed in whatever we do."[9]

Christian obedience is obedience to the Lord Jesus Christ (I Peter 1:2), not obedience to a book. Nowhere in scripture is a Christian encouraged to obey some "thing" such as a book. What kind of a "blessing" does one get from a book? Paul indicates that "God ... has blessed us with every spiritual blessing in the heavenlies in Christ" (Ephesians 1:3).

"His (Christ's) perfect wisdom is available through His Word (Bible)."[10]

Paul explicitly tells the Corinthians that as Christians who have received the Spirit of God, they have wisdom. "Christ is our wisdom" (I Corinthians 1:24,30).

"If you're a Christian...you need the Word (Bible) for training and spiritual growth."[11]

What about Christians who do not have the Bible translated into their language, or those who cannot read a book even if were available? Spiritual growth is by the Spirit of God, not by book-knowledge.

If that were not enough, MacArthur goes on to attribute to the Bible what can only be attributed to God in Christ concerning the regeneration of men.

"The Word of God (Bible) is perfectly able to open an unbeliever's eyes to the truth of the gospel, convict him of sin, or even do radical surgery on his soul."[12]

Jesus Christ carefully explained to the disciples that He was going to go away and would send the Holy Spirit who would "convict the world concerning sin, and righteousness, and judgment" (John 16:8). The Holy Spirit "convicts of sin," not the Bible itself.

"Scripture itself is...adequate for evangelism"[13]

MacArthur implies this by referring to "liberalism's legacy" that "Scripture itself is inadequate for evangelism.." Jesus said that He would "draw all men to Himself" (John 12:32). How then can scripture "itself" be adequate for evangelism?

"He (Jesus) knew the saving power of God's Word (Bible)."[14]

"Paul was certain that God's Word (Bible) itself was sufficient to provoke true saving faith in the hardest unbeliever's hearts."[15]

"God's Word (Bible) is the seed that produces salvation."[16]

"If you're not a Christian.....you need the Word (Bible) for salvation."[17]

"Scripture imparts salvation."[18]

How can any Christian with any degree of knowledge of the scriptures make such statements? God's saving power is in His Son, Jesus Christ, not in the Bible. The Bible "itself" is not sufficient to provoke saving faith; God alone provokes such. Salvation is produced only by the action of the Savior, Jesus Christ, not the Bible. Salvation is not some "thing" imparted or dispensed; rather it is the ongoing saving activity of Jesus Christ our Savior.

But the real clincher of misunderstanding is evident when MacArthur states:

"Believing God's Word (Bible) results in eternal life."[19]

What did Jesus say? He said to the Jews, "You search the Scriptures, because you think that in them you have eternal life; and it is these that bear witness of Me" (John 5:39). Later Jesus prayed, "this is eternal life, that they may know Thee, the only true God, and Jesus Christ whom Thou hast sent" (John 17:3). John MacArthur, Jr. has apparently placed himself in the company of Judaistic Pharisaism!

Robert P. Lightner, professor of theology at Dallas Theological Seminary, has made similar assertions concerning the Scriptures:

"The Written Word and the Living Word...(as the article is entitled)...These Words from God (Scripture and Jesus Christ) are two impregnable forces, the pillars upon which Christianity stands or falls."[20]

What does he mean that the Bible is a "force"? Jesus Christ, by His Spirit, might be said to be a "force," i.e. to have

43

power, God's divine power, but how can a written volume of a book have "force" or divine power? There are not two pillars on which Christianity stands. Christianity IS Christ! Christianity is the dynamic of Christ's life functioning in His people; not some "thing" that stands on two pillars. Such an assertion as Lightner makes is tantamount to making the equation that "Christianity = Christ + Bible." That is an abominable falsehood. Throughout Paul's writings, and particularly in Galatians and Colossians, Paul indicates that the Christian gospel is Jesus Christ alone; "Christianity = Christ + (nothing)."

> "These two (Written Word and Living Word) are inseparable from each other and from biblical Christianity."[21]

To state that Jesus Christ and the Bible are "inseparable" is to equate the book with Jesus Christ. Only Jesus Christ is "inseparable" from Christianity, for Christianity IS Christ.

> "The Written Word of God and the living Son of God...both unquestionably constitute divine revelation from Him."[22]

> "God's Written Word...reveals the person and work of God while at the same time it is His own divine revelation."[23]

Jesus Christ alone, as the living Word of God, reveals the Father. Jesus said, "No one knows the Father, except the Son, and anyone to whom the Son wills to reveal Him

(Matthew 11:27). Only God as Father, Son and Holy Spirit can reveal Himself. It is a personal revelation, not an impersonal revelation. The book called the Bible does not "constitute" divine revelation. God constitutes the revelation of Himself.

> "Both Words (Living and Written) claim the same authority."[24]

> "The Written Word is as eternal as God and therefore as authoritative as God Himself."[25]

To thus equate the Living Word, Jesus, with the written scriptures is to deify the book. The attributes of God cannot be attributed to created matter. Divine attributes such as eternality and authority must not be attributed to the Bible as Lightner has done.

> "The authority which He (Jesus Christ) claimed for Himself and the authority which He claimed for the Scriptures is identical."[26]

Jesus does not claim authority for scripture identical to His own authority. Jesus claimed exclusive authority when He said, "All authority is given to Me in heaven and on earth" (Matthew 38:18).

> "......to receive one (Written Word or Living Word) is to receive both."[27]

45

What an outlandish and heretical assertion to claim that to receive the Bible is to receive Jesus Christ! One can only give mental assent to sentential statements and propositional premises of written material in a book. To receive Jesus Christ involves spiritual receptivity of faith, which is far more than mental assent.

> "Invariably, those who reject the Bible as God's Written Word also reject Jesus Christ as the Living Word."   "...to reject one is to reject both..."[28]

The first statement is an overly inclusive assumption. The second statement is simply fallacious. The continued capitalization of "Written Word" in reference to the Bible alongside of "Living Word" in reference to Jesus Christ, evidences the author's deification of the scriptures.

> "Perhaps our devotion to the Written Word sometimes gives the impression that we are worshipping a book..."[29]

It most certainly does! If the author means what he says by the words that he uses, then he is indeed guilty of bibliolatrous worship of the Bible. The "devotion" of our worship is to be directed toward God alone. "God is Spirit, and we are to worship Him in spirit and in truth" (John 4:24).

46

Fundamentalist authors such as MacArthur and Lightner have assumed fallacious presuppositions of thought. They make invalid equations of numerous ideas and words with the Bible: "word" (whether *logos* or *rhema*) = Bible; "law" = Bible; "commandment" = Bible; "ordinance" = Bible; "teaching" = Bible; "doctrine"= Bible; "authority" = Bible; "revelation" = Bible; "truth" = Bible; "precept" = Bible; "testimony" = Bible; "preaching" = Bible; "gospel" = Bible; "Holy Spirit" = Bible; "Christ" = Bible. These authors read through the scriptures, and whenever they find these words or concepts they eisegetically presuppose that it is referring to the Bible.

These authors often equate the action of God the Father, Son and Holy Spirit with the Bible. Attributes of the Godhead are transferred to the Bible. Attributes such as eternality, absoluteness, authority, power, sufficiency for living, truth, life, wisdom, righteousness, holiness, faith, salvation, exaltation and inerrancy are all attributed to the scriptures. To do so is to deify the Bible. To thus elevate the scriptures is to engage in the superstitious mysticism of bibliolatry. To attribute to a book, to attribute to any "thing" or anyone, what is only attributable to God is to engage in idolatry. God's attributes are essential, exclusive

47

and non-transferrable. God is the only One who is who He is and does what He does, as expressed in His attributes. Only God is God! To attribute God's attributes to a book is to make the book a "god," and to relativize God's attributes. Persons who hold such a view of scripture need to do a thorough study of the attributes of God and to recognize that these are attributes of God alone! Heresy usually commences with a deficient understanding of God.

Historical Review of Biblical Understanding

By reviewing biblical history we can gain some perspective of how God expresses Himself. God is a God who must express Himself as who He is. His prime function is active expression of Himself consistent with His character. He is the living, active God who personally expresses Himself.

God expressed Himself in creation by etiologically expressing "out of" Himself (Cf. Romans 11:33; I Corinthians 8:6) a created order that was not essentially divine (pantheism), but expressive of His own character. This *ek theos* process of creative Self-expression was for the purpose of allowing His invisible character to be expressed visibly in His creation, to His own glory.

48

This was God's intent for man when He created mankind with the "image of God" in man (Genesis 1:26,27). The expressive agent of God, the Son, the "Word," was to "image" God's character in the behavior of man. "Christ, the image of God" (II Corinthians 4:4; Colossians 1:15) was to be the spiritual resource for imaging God's character within godly behavior in man, manifesting "godliness," to the glory of God.

The expressive agency of the living, personal God (that is the Word, the Image of God, the Son) in man was lost in the fall of man in sin (cf. Gen. 3). That does not mean that God ceased to express Himself, though, for to cease to express Himself, He would cease to be God. But as God's intent was to express Himself in the highest form of His creation, i.e. in man, for a glorification of His character that was not possible in the lower created orders without behavioral freedom, God's ultimate purpose was temporarily thwarted by sin.

On Sinai there was given to Moses an enscribed law, engraved and written on stone, the purpose of which was to reveal God's intention of expressing His character in man through the expressive agent of His Son, Jesus Christ. All Old Testament law and function points to Jesus Christ.

Men being men (natural systematizers, categorizers, formulizers, moralizers and theologizers) took the enscribed law and made it into a textualized book-religion. Men foolishly think that a written record can contain, or can adequately describe and define the Living Word expression of God. The natural tendency of man is to think that if they see it in print, it is to be taken as gospel. Men take that which is of God and attempt to objectify, tangibilize and absolutize. God can never be contained in some "thing," including a book. When men think that the expression of God is contained in a book, it becomes mere sacramentalism.

Judaism became a book-religion based on the textualized Torah and reinforced by rigid, written tradition. Rabbinic theologizing and moralizing became inflexible and legalistic. Jewish religion centered around exegeting, interpreting and implementing precisely the truth of the Torah text, precept upon precept (Isaiah 28:10,13). The minutia of the written record became absolutized. The Torah and its traditions were regarded as eternal, inerrant and absolute. Religious reverence and allegiance to the Torah became idolatry. They had made an idol out of the

Law and were worshipping the Book, the Law, the Torah, rather than God.

The stage was set for the showdown confrontation between Judaic and Pharisaic book-religion and the personal, living Word of God expressed incarnate in Jesus Christ. John's gospel narrative, known as "the spiritual gospel," was intended to be the antidote which would prevent early Christianity from falling victim to the deadly trait of textualism. The apostle John begins his writing, "In the beginning was the Word and the Word was with God, and the Word was God. He was in the beginning with God" (John 1:1,2). "The Word became flesh, and dwelt among us, and we beheld His glory, glory as of the only begotten from the Father, full of grace and truth" (John 1:14). Who is the Word who is eternal, inerrant, Divine expression? Jesus Christ! The "Who", the personal Word, Jesus Christ, confronted the "what", the written record of words that Jewish religionists regarded as eternal, inerrant, divine expression.

Jesus explained to the Jews, "You do not have His word abiding in you, for you do not believe Him whom He sent. You search the Scriptures, because you think that in them you have eternal life; and it is these that bear witness of

51

Me; and you are unwilling to come to Me, that you may have life" (John 5:38-40). The scribal Pharisees "searched the scriptures," they stalked the game, traced the tracks, counted the syllables, but they could not fathom that the Word of God, the Life of God, the Truth of God was in a Person, rather than in written propositions or sentential statements. They insisted on playing Torah-trivia games. There was a perverse unwillingness to accept Jesus Christ as the source of all life. Coming from their perspective of book-religion, they could not accommodate into their thinking, and would not receive Jesus Christ as the Living Word of God. They chose to stick with their "picture-book;" to peruse the catalogue rather than receiving that which it pictured.

When Jesus came in the flesh, He did not come teaching like the scribes, proscribing and prescribing from written texts. He did not come imparting information for a revised belief-system. He was not like the temple theologians with their abstract theological theses. Jesus told stories. He painted parabolic pictures of commonplace phenomena. He knew that the living, dynamic expression of God was in Himself and could not be contained in precise doctrinal definition, in sentential semantics, in theological treatises.

Jesus did not write anything as far as we know, except, perhaps, a few words in the sand as He pondered the perversity of the scribes and Pharisees in the midst of their "set-up" with the adulterous woman (John 8:6). As the living Word of God, He expressed divine character and truth. Again to the Jews, Jesus said, "the words that I have spoken to you are spirit and are life" (John 6:63).

As He neared the conclusion of His physical, earthly ministry in the upper room with the disciples, Jesus did not tell them that He would leave them a written text of scriptures to take His place and to reveal all they needed to know. Rather, Jesus told His disciples,

> "I will ask the Father, and He will give you another (just like Me) Encourager, that He may be with you forever; the Spirit of Truth, whom the world cannot receive, because it does not behold Him or know Him, but you know Him because He abides with you, and will be in you" (John 14:16,17).

Jesus continued by saying,

> "If anyone loves Me, he will keep My word; and My Father will love him, and We will come to him and make Our abode with him. He who does not love Me does not keep My words; and the word which you hear is not Mine, but the Father's who sent Me. These things I have spoken to you, while abiding with you. But the Encourager, the Holy Spirit, whom the Father will send in My

name, He will teach you all things, and bring to your remembrance all that I said to you" (John 14:23-26).

It is not the Bible that is to "teach us all things." The Spirit of Christ, the Holy Spirit, the continuing personal expression of God to man, the Word indwelling in us teaches us all things and expresses God in man. Every Christian has the indwelling presence of the Word, Jesus Christ, or else that person is not a Christian.

> "You have an anointing from the Holy One, and you all know" (I John 2:20). "The anointing which you received from Him abides in you, and you have no need for anyone to teach you; but as His anointing teaches you about all things, and is true and is not a lie, and just as it (He) has taught you, you abide in Him" (I John 2:27).

Can you see the problem the Jewish scribes and Pharisees had with Jesus? Jesus came claiming to personally BE all that they ascribed to the precepts of the law and commandments of the Torah. Jesus came saying, "I AM the Word, the Life, the Light, the Truth, the Wisdom, the Way, etc.

The living expression of God can never be codified in the definitions and descriptions of written words. Such is the anomaly of Christianity. Could this be what John meant in the very last word of his gospel narrative when he wrote, "there are also many other things which Jesus did, which if they were written in detail, I suppose that even the world

54

itself would not contain the books which were written" (John 21:25). The world could not contain the books if man even attempted to reduce to writing the expression of God in Jesus Christ, which is, of course, impossible. The activity of God cannot be reduced to volumes written in the vocabularies of man. The apostle John was combating the tendency of textualism in the early church.

The historical story continues. Jesus, the living expression of God, the Word, was crucified in order to take our death that we might have His life. His death did not silence the living expression of God. It only served as the nuclear fusion to explode God's expression unto all men. For in the resurrection, ascension and Pentecostal outpouring of Jesus Christ by the Spirit, the personal, living expression of God, His Word, could spiritually indwell all mankind as they received Him by faith, man's receptivity of God's activity.

The early Christians were not propagating a belief-system. They were not dispensers of theological information about God. They were not Book-bearers. They were bearers of the Living Word, the Life, the Person, the Power of Jesus, "who is the Spirit" (II Corinthians 3:18).

Paul had to correct the Galatians and the Corinthians when they were misinformed by Judaizing legalists, propagating book-religion. Jesus came to fulfill the law (Matthew 5:17), not by providing an impersonal impetus of additional commitment to help men to perform it, but by His own indwelling expression to be the "law written on our hearts" (Hebrews 8:10; 10:16) – the divine law-expresser, character-expresser in us. To the Galatians Paul wrote, "if you are led by the Spirit (all Christians are), you are not under the Law" (Galatians 5:18). To the Corinthians Paul wrote,

> "Not that we are adequate in ourselves to consider anything as coming from ourselves, but our adequacy is from God, who also made us adequate as servants of a new covenant, not of the letter, but of the Spirit; for the letter kills, but the Spirit gives life. But if the ministry of death, in letters engraved on stones, came with glory, so that the sons of Israel could not look intently at the face of Moses because of the glory of his face, fading as it was, how shall the ministry of the Spirit fail to be even more with glory? (II Corinthians 3:5-8)

From an autobiographical perspective Paul shared with the Romans,

> "we have been released from the Law, having died to that by which we were bound, so that we serve in newness of the Spirit and not in oldness of the letter. What shall we say then? Is the Law sin? May it never be! On the contrary, I would not have come to know sin except through the Law; for I would not have known about coveting if the Law had not said, 'You shall not covet.' But sin,

56

taking opportunity through the commandment, produced in me coveting of every kind; for apart from the Law sin is dead. And I was once alive apart from the Law; but when the commandment came, sin became alive, and I died; and this commandment, which was to result in life, proved to result in death for me; for sin, taking opportunity through the commandment, deceived me, and through it killed me." (Romans 7:6-11)

When we operate by the letter of the law, a written code of conduct, all it does is make hypocrites of us. We cannot perform according to the standards contained therein; only Jesus can, for He is the expresser of the character of God in man.

In the early church most of the Christians were simple, illiterate people. Many were from slave backgrounds and could not read or write. It is estimated that as many as eighty-percent of the early Christians were illiterate. Most were Gentiles with no Bible-background. They possessed no Bibles as either individual or community property. The Old Testament papyrus scrolls were, for the most part, maintained at the synagogue and were not "on loan" to the Christian congregations. In the early decades of the church what we know as the New Testament had not been written yet.

What did the early Christians do when they assembled together? I am convinced that they did not do what we so often *do* when we gather together. Today, evangelical

57

Christians assemble together to *do* Bible study. It is sort of a "Bible Information Clinic" where one teacher gets up to "throw the Book at you." Hebrews 10:24,25 indicates that the early Christians assembled together to "encourage" one another, not just to *do* something exegetically and interpretively and motivationally from the written word. They came together to share with one another what the Living Word, the Spirit of Christ, was *doing* in them; how God was expressing Himself in them in their daily lives.

Jesus did not say, "I am the object of Bible information, and you shall know it most thoroughly and accurately." Rather, He said, "I am the Way, the Truth and the Life" (John 14:6); "I came that you might have Life and have it most abundantly" (John 10:10).

What if there were no Bibles? What if the New Testament had never been written, or never been preserved, or never been canonized? What if all the Bibles were destroyed from the face of the earth today? Should that make any difference to Christianity? It should not! Christianity IS Christ, the dynamic life of Jesus Christ, the spiritual indwelling of God whereby He expresses Himself, His character, in the highest of His creation unto His own glory. The absence of the book would not forestall what

Jesus said, "Upon this rock I will build My church, and the gates of Hades shall not overpower it" (Matthew 16:18). God's preservation of His people, His church, is not contingent or dependent on our knowing the factual data of a book. It is not what we "do"; it is what God "does" by His expression, His living Word, Jesus Christ in us.

Within the context of the early church a written record did materialize and come into being. There were gospel narratives recording how the Living Word, Jesus Christ, appeared in flesh. Paul and others wrote epistles encouraging Christians to allow for the dynamic expression of Christ in them. These writings were compiled into what we know as the New Testament. For all the benefit that these writings have had as an objective criteria of Christian understanding, there has been the counteractive risk whereby the natural propensity of man tends to develop absolutism, textualism and legalism, and thus to allow Christianity to become a "religion of the book."

Robert Brinsmead of Australia writes,

"The written record became absolutized. The gospel became a new law. Faith was confounded with orthodoxy. The Church ceased to be a charismatic community and became an institution. Instead of the Spirit there were rules. Instead of the priesthood of all believers, there was wretched clericalism. Instead of the Spirit and presence of the living Christ there were religious canned goods.

Instead of the living gospel there was dead ideology. Instead of freedom there was bondage. Yet, like the Pharisees, we have desperately tried to substitute an incredible devotion to the letter of Scripture for the prophetic spirit."[30]

Jumping many centuries, we arrive in our historical survey at the religious Reformation of the sixteenth century. Roman Catholicism insisted on the inerrancy and infallibility of the Pope; the authority was vested in the Church and its papal proclamations. The Protestants insisted on the inerrancy and infallibility of the Bible; the authority *of sola scriptura*. Despite these contradictory claims for the basis of authority, Jesus said, "All authority is given to Me, in heaven and on earth" (Matthew 28:18). Inerrancy and infallibility is inherent in the living expression of God in Christ, and in Him alone. The Roman Catholics were susceptible (and still are) to ecclesiolatry, idolatrous worship of the church institution. The Protestants were susceptible (and still are) to bibliolatry, idolatrous worship of the Bible. In fact, the Catholics chided the Protestants for having a "paper pope" and a "God who was imprisoned in a book." At least the Catholic conception of God and pope was "personal," though mere man.

The Protestant Reformation fostered static concepts of *sola scriptura*, justification, salvation, grace, faith, worship,

60

etc. All branches of Protestantism down through the centuries have prided themselves on being "the people of the Book" or "the religion of the Book." G.K. Chesterton once wrote,

"The Bible and the Bible only is the religion of the Protestants."[31]

Bringing the historical survey up to date, we have just witnessed a couple of decades of evangelical conflict and debate. "The Battle for the Bible" has been the issue. There have been volumes of books and articles on inerrancy, infallibility and inspiration of scripture. They miss the point! What about proclaiming the eternal, inerrant, infallible inspiration of Jesus Christ, the Living Word expression of God, in people's lives? We need a Christocentric Christianity rather than a bibliocentric Christian religion. Christianity IS Christ!

This was intended to be but a brief historical review emphasizing God's intent to express Himself in Living Word in Jesus Christ. But as we note how man constantly attempts to revert to book-religion, it becomes a long story of religious perversion.

Man always grasps for a visible, physical, tangible object that he can "hold on to." Men seem to want

61

something visible instead of invisible, tangible instead of intangible, physical instead of spiritual, concrete instead of abstract, some "thing" instead of Some One, an object instead of the Living God. These objects are then made into idols. It is done with the Bible just as with other kinds of objects. When this happens it is called "bibliolatry," idolatrous worship of the Bible. It can take the form of merely an undue reverence for a leather-covered book. For some, the book becomes a sort of magical fetish, a "good-luck" charm, supposedly offering spirituality by osmosis. Sometimes bibliolatry is evidenced in an excessive literalistic method of interpretation that fails to account for varying types of Biblical literature.

We must beware of regarding the Bible as a "sacred" book, having some kind of saving significance in itself. Even the title on the cover of most Bibles needs to be clarified – "Holy Bible." Is the Holy Bible holy? Holiness is an attribute of God alone. A created object is not holy in itself and does not convey holiness. When an object is used for the purpose that God intended then that object can serve God's holy purposes. When it is set apart to function as intended, it can serve the holy purposes of God directed toward the divine objective to manifest His holiness by the presence of His Holy Son, Jesus Christ in us. But the book itself is not intrinsically holy. We need to make sure we understand why it is called a "Holy Bible."

We do not want to be guilty of bibliolatry or the biblicism of mere book-religion. Jesus never intended Christianity to be a book-religion, rigidly controlled by textual research, Biblical exegesis and motivation to implement Scriptural principles and precepts. Such was not the case in the early church, as has been indicated above. They did not gather together to *do* Bible study, but to share how the living expression of the Word of God in Jesus Christ was operative and functioning in their lives. They shared with one another what God was *doing* and expressing in them.

It becomes apparent that we have lapsed into an inappropriate teaching model in the evangelical churches of America today. We have become book-centered, teacher-controlled and educationally-oriented. It might be called "the poisonous pedagogy of ecclesiasticism," the perpetual propagation of a belief-system. Bible knowledge is often regarded as an "end" in itself. Paul is clear that "knowledge puffeth up" (I Corinthians 8:1); mere knowledge, including

Bible knowledge, creates arrogance, pride, hypocrisy and the like.

Book-religion creates a mechanistic system, a belief-system or ethical-system. Such systematized religion depersonalizes and devitalizes God, as well as dehumanizing man. We are not functional humanity as God intended unless the Living expression of the Word of God in Jesus Christ is functioning in us.

A Biblical Understanding of the Bible

The purpose of the Bible is not to serve as a book of rules and regulations, ethical guidelines fixed in the concrete of moralistic legalism. The Bible is not an ethics book. The Bible is not a textbook of proof-texts to defend Christian doctrine as it has been systematized by man. You can attempt to prove almost anything from the Bible. (I recall one individual who maintained that it was wrong to peel a banana on the basis of the reading "whatsoever God has put together, let no man part asunder.") The Bible is not a law or logic textbook to prove one's point. It is not a textbook of theological trivia. The Bible is not a sociological textbook that settles the institutional church into the conservatism of the status-quo. The Bible is not an encyclopedic text that gives every answer to every question on every subject in the universe. This is not the purpose of the Bible.

What then is the purpose of the Bible? The purpose of the Bible is to bear witness to Jesus Christ, who is the living expression of God, the Word of God. Jesus told the Jews,

> "...you do not have His word abiding in you, for you do not believe Him whom He sent. You search the Scriptures, because you think that in them you have eternal life; and it is these that bear witness of Me; and you are unwilling to come to Me, that you may have life." (John 5:38-40)

The Scriptures bear witness of Jesus. A good witness in a judicial setting does not focus attention on himself, but to the issue at hand. The Biblical writings do not point to themselves, but to Jesus Christ. The written record of God's expression and revelation of Himself in Jesus Christ is designed to direct a person to faith in Jesus Christ, to receptivity of the redemptive and functionally living activity of Jesus Christ.

The apostle John explains the purpose of his writing the gospel narrative attributed to him: "these have been written that you may believe that Jesus is the Christ, the Son of God; and that believing you may have life in His name"

(John 20:31). The purpose of the Scriptures is to lead one to receive the life that is in Christ Jesus.

The apostle Paul reminds Timothy of the value of the written record, urging him to "continue in the things you have learned and become convinced of, knowing from whom you have learned them; and that from childhood you have known the sacred writings which are able to give you the wisdom that leads to salvation through faith which is in Christ Jesus" (II Timothy 3:14,15). The translation reads "sacred writings," but there is no intrinsic sacredness or holiness in the writings themselves, as has been previously noted. Paul was simply referring to the "God-given writings." The purpose of the writings is that they are "able to give...wisdom..." The God-given writings serve as a vehicle, an instrument, that the Spirit of God uses to impart the spiritual wisdom and discernment necessary to understand spiritual things in order that one might see their need for functionally restorative salvation, which comes only by the receptivity of the activity of the Savior, Jesus Christ. The Scriptures serve an instrumental means, but are not a salvific means in themselves.

Paul continues his words to Timothy by explaining, "all Scripture is inspired by God and profitable for teaching, for reproof, for correction, for training in righteousness; that the man of God may be adequate, equipped for every good work." (II Timothy 3:16,17) What did Paul mean by "all Scripture?" Could Paul have been referring to the scriptures we call the New Testament, in that they were still in the process of being written? When Christians today refer to the "Scripture" they usually have a very fixated conception of a particular bound volume entitled "The Holy Bible" with sixty-six books, thirty-nine in the Old Testament and twenty-seven in the New Testament. As there was no such book in Paul's time, it is inconceivable that Paul was thinking of such an approved canonized collection of writings. The words that Paul uses are more generic. In verse fifteen where Paul refers to the "writings," it is a translation of the Greek word *gramma*, from which we get the English word "grammar." This word simply referred to written lettering using the letters of the alphabet. In verse sixteen, the word "Scripture" is a translation of the Greek word *graphe*, from which we get the English word "graphics." This word simply referred to something written. The Latin word *scriptus* translated the Greek word *graphe*, and thus it was that the Latin *scriptura* became the designation of the "writings" used by Christians, and eventually of the canonized collection of what we know as the sixty-six books of the Bible, the Scriptures.

Paul is indicating that certain "writings" are "God-breathed," that is "inspired." This does not mean that God breathed out verbal words to dictate every word and sentence in precise and absolute sequence unto the passive minds of the writers. Such a concept is called the "dictation theory" of scriptural inspiration. Rather, in a more general sense, Paul seems to be saying that "all God-given writings are designed as the expressive instrument of God's Spirit, who functioned previously to influence men's thinking and use their literary skills to produce and provide a written record of the expressed life of God in Jesus Christ, and functions now to continue to direct us to the ever-dynamic life of Christ." These writings, whether they be of the Old Testament era or the New Testament era, are valuable and profitable for teaching, reproof, correction and training in righteousness. The importance of the "writings" is that they direct our attention to the Living Word expression of God in Jesus Christ.

The question must be asked then: Is it legitimate to refer to the written record of the Bible as the "Word of God"? When we refer to the Bible as the "Word of God" does this not create a duplicated ambiguity of terminology? (Yes, I know that I am treading on the sacred ground of bibliolatry, but I must press on!) On what basis do we refer to the Bible as the "Word of God"? Is there anything within the Bible itself that says that we are to refer to this book in its collected totality as the "Word of God"? Is there any Biblical justification for that designation?

I encourage you to make the same observations that I did when I looked at an English concordance of the Bible and searched out all the references to the word "word" and, more specifically, references to the "word of God." Valid exegetical analysis does not indicate that a single usage of the phrase, "word of God," ever refers to the book that we call "The Bible."

To further explore the basis of this popular designation of the "word of God," I examined several Bible dictionaries and encyclopedias looking up the subject of the "word of God." To my amazement, not a one of them indicated that the phrase referred to the Bible or the Scriptures. Rather, they all explained that Jesus Christ is the personified expression of God, the "Word" (John 1:1,14), and went on to explain that the proclamation of God's expression in Jesus Christ is the essence of the gospel. The good news of the gospel is the "word" (Matt. 13:19; Col. 4:3; I Peter 3:1), the "word of God" (Acts 4:31; I Cor. 14:36; Phil. 1:14; I Thess. 2:13), the "word of truth" (II Timothy 2:15), the "word of life" (Phil. 2:16), the "word of reconciliation" (II Corinthians 5:19), the "word of salvation" (Acts 13:26), or the "word of faith" (Romans 10:8).

How can it be that we have been so thoroughly propagandized by the Judeo-Christian book-religion, that we so unquestioningly refer to the Bible as the "word of God," and mistakenly identify most references within Scripture to the "word" as references to the Bible instead of to Jesus Christ or to the gospel of Christ? Book-religion is very pervasive!

None of those who wrote, by the inspired divine influence of God, the writings that now comprise the compilation of writings that we call the Bible; none of them apparently ever conceived that their writings would be collected and canonized into a book called "The Bible" or "The Scriptures," which would then be referred to as the "Word of God." That is not to say that they were not aware of God's influence in their writing, but whenever they refer to the "word" (either *logos* or *rhema*), or to the "writings" (either *gramma* or *graphe*), or to the scrolls or books (*biblion*), it is not a reference to the totality of the bound-book that we call the Bible. We need to be honest enough to admit that!

Some common Biblical examples will serve to demonstrate the point I have been making:

Romans 10:17 - "So faith comes from hearing, and hearing by the word of Christ." "Word of Christ" in this text does not refer to Bible knowledge. The context has to do with the verbalized proclamation of the gospel.

Galatians 6:6 - "let the one who is taught the word share all good things with him who teaches." The "word" is not a reference to Bible doctrine or narratives, but refers to the gospel.

Ephesians 6:17 - "the sword of the Spirit, which is the word of God." How often have we heard the Bible referred to as the "word of God" and the "sword of the Spirit"? This verse is not referring to a bound-book, but to the personalized word of God which God speaks to the Christian.

Colossians 3:16 - "Let the word of Christ richly dwell within you..." Paul is not saying, "let the words of the Bible" dwell in you. The parallel passage in Ephesians 5:18

explains that the Spirit of Christ is to fill us and dwell within us.

Colossians 4:3 - "praying ... that God may open up to us a door for the word, so that we may speak forth the mystery of Christ..." Again, Paul is referring to the gospel, not to the Bible.

II Timothy 4:2 - "preach the word..." Paul admonishes Timothy to preach the gospel of Christ, not Biblical information.

Hebrews 4:12 - "For the word of God is living and active and sharper than any two-edged sword, and piercing as far as the division of soul and spirit, of both joints and marrow, and able to judge the thoughts and intentions of the heart." Jesus Christ by the Spirit is that "word of God" which is living and active and able to penetrate into our being. A textualized book is unable to do so.

If anyone should choose to refer to the Bible, the collected Scriptures, as the "Word of God," it should be remembered that such a designation can only be made in a secondary sense. The primary and absolute sense of the "Word of God" is in the expression of God in His Son, Jesus Christ. Jesus is the eternal Word of God expressed in creation, expressed in redemption, expressed in sanctification, expressed in glorification.

The Bible is not the "Word of God" in an absolute sense. It is a book comprised of a compilation of "words" about the Word of God, Jesus Christ. Jesus Himself said, "The Scriptures bear witness of Me" (John 5:39). The written words point to the Living Word, Jesus Christ. In fact, the Bible does not even "contain" the Word of God, for such would be sacramentalism. The Living Word of God, Jesus Christ, cannot be imprisoned in a book. He must be free to express Himself as God in man, and that unto the functionally free humanity through which God intends to glorify Himself.

As Jesus thus expresses Himself in us, by His Spirit, He will bear inner testimony in our spirit, and unto our minds, of the value of the Book, the Bible, in our lives. Apart from this illumination and enlightenment, the personal revelation of the Spirit of Christ, the spiritual insights, the living characterization factors that are to be gained from the Biblical literature will never be appreciated anyway.

The Spirit of God uses the Scripture preserved for us by God. The Living Word of God uses the written words of God. Jesus Christ uses the Bible to reveal how it is that He wants to function in us to reveal God in man. This is why we noted at the outset that the Bible is in one sense like every other book in the world: written words, literature, a bound-book. But in another sense the Bible is unlike every other book in the world. The Living Word, Jesus, uses this book to reveal how it is He has functioned and continues to function as God in man.

The "natural man" does not understand spiritual things" (I Corinthians 2:14) regardless of how many times he might attempt to read the words of the Bible. Jesus told His disciples, "when He, the Spirit of truth, comes, He will guide you into all the truth.." (John 16:13). The Spirit of Christ, Who is Truth (John 14:6), may utilize the Bible to reveal and disclose Himself, but He does not require the written book in order to do so. The Teacher is not tied to the text! The Spirit is not bound in the Bible!

Apart from the Living Word, Jesus Christ, functioning spiritually in our lives, the book is mere "letter" (legalistic biblicism), and there is no Spirit-action, no genuine divine functioning. To the Corinthians Paul wrote, "God... made us adequate as servants of a new covenant, not of the letter, but of the Spirit; for the letter kills, but the Spirit gives life." (II Corinthians 3:6,7). Mere book-religion kills, but

Spirit-revelation gives life. Mere comprehension of Bible-words kills, but the Spirit of Christ, the Living Word of God, gives life. To the Romans Paul wrote, "we have been released from the Law, having died to that by which we were bound, so that we serve in newness of the Spirit and not in oldness of the letter" (Romans 7:6). Christians are not "bound" to the "letter" of book-religion. We live and serve in the newness of the Spirit of Christ activating our lives from within.

Without the indwelling of the Spirit of Christ, reading the Bible will be like reading someone else's mail. You cannot understand it because it was not intended for you. Oh, you may be able to chart the history. You may be able to discuss the theology. You might even be able to produce detailed speculations about the future, but you will not be able to receive the living, spiritual implications of the life of Jesus Christ. This is why Martin Luther indicated that if your spiritual condition is that of the unregenerate, being devoid of the Spirit, you are better off reading some other book! That is also why it is said, "the Bible is the only book in the world that requires knowing the Author to understand the book." One must "know" and have a personal relationship with the Living Word expression of

God in Jesus Christ in order to spiritually understand the written word expression of God in the Bible.

As Christians today, coming as many of us do out of a Protestant tradition of biblicism, it is important that we keep our perspective properly focused on the Person of Jesus Christ, not just on Bible-learning. Jesus Christ is the Truth, not mere propositional truths contained in ever-evolving semantics.

Our faith is not in the Bible. Our hope is not in the Bible. Our love is not love for the Bible. Our faith, hope and love are in Jesus Christ.

Our base of authority is not in the Bible, as has often been projected by popular Protestantism, the "religion of the Book." Our base of authority is in Jesus Christ, who said, "All authority is given to Me, in heaven and upon earth" (Matthew 28:18).

Our security is not in the Bible. Many seem to base their security on Bible promises and propositions, on Bible formulas, procedures and techniques. Our security is founded on a vital, dynamic on-going personal relationship with the Living Lord Jesus Christ. I am assured and secure in the reality that God is expressive in my life by Jesus Christ. I know it, not because the Bible makes a statement ("the Bible tells me so") or gives me a procedure. I know it (Him) because the eternal life and eternal expression of Jesus Christ is functioning in my life. This is not mere experiential existentialism. Somewhere between the extremes of objective biblicism and subjective existentialism is the reality of the functional Life of Jesus Christ in man.

As Christians we want to know Jesus as the Word of God, the expression of God in man, rather than just words from a book. We want to experience the Person of Jesus, not just examine the photograph, the picture, that represents the reality. We want to be sheep who hear His voice, the voice of the Shepherd, not just sheep who "feed" on the fodder of theological canned goods, or Scriptural scrapings.

The Life of Jesus Christ who is the Living expression of God, the Living Word, is to be expressed in gospel proclamation that shares the "word of truth," the "word of life," the "word of salvation." II Timothy 3:16 indicates that "all scripture/writings are profitable for teaching, for reproof, for correction, for training in righteousness, that the man of God may be adequately equipped for every good work" (which God prepared beforehand that we should walk in them - Ephesians 2:10). It is true that the

77

Bible is to be taught, and that God has gifted some as teachers (Ephesians 4:11; I Corinthians 12:28; Romans 12:7), but the process of Biblical instruction (teaching) and the product of the instruction (Bible-knowledge), must not become ends in themselves. It appears that there has been the perpetuation of a poisonous and counter-productive pedagogy in evangelical ecclesiasticism, a "teaching model" that perpetuates book-religion, Bible knowledge, and getting "fed" through Scripture instruction. This creates dysfunctional Christianity, mere Christian-religion, which does not issue forth in the outworking expression of Christ's life.

Christianity is not a book-religion! Christianity is Christ functioning as the expressive revelation and Word of God in man.

Chapter Three

CHRISTIANITY IS *NOT* MORALITY

A major television network was filming a documentary on "Christian fundamentalism." They were interviewing a young couple exiting a fundamentalist church. The interviewer asked, "What do Christian fundamentalists believe?" The conservatively dressed respondent replied, "We believe in the Bible. We don't believe in drinking, smoking or dancing. We try to be as good as we can to please God." What a tragic misrepresentation of Christianity. Yet this is the misconception being propagated in the name of "Christianity." Is it any wonder that few are interested?

The average man on the street believes that Christianity is a religion that imposes a particular morality with specific ethical behavior. He has concluded that "a Christian is one who lives by certain rules and regulations imposed upon him by divine or ecclesiastically dictated 'thou shalts' and 'thou shalt nots,' and that behavioral conformity to these moral codes of conduct is what the Christian strives to perform in order to please and/or appease God." The tragic part of this misconception is that Christian religion has "faked" the world into believing that such is the essence of Christianity.

The French social analyst, Jacques Ellul noted this misrepresentative tendency:

> "In the eyes of most of our contemporaries, Christianity is a morality first of all. And have not many epochs of Christian history been characterized by the church's insistence upon actions and conduct?"[1]

> "We have to recognize that Christians themselves have done all they can to create this confusion. God's revelation has nothing whatever to do with morality."[2]

C.S. Lewis similarly explained,

> "I think all Christians would agree with me if I said that though Christianity seems at first to be all about morality, all about duties and rules and guilt and virtue, yet it leads you on, out of all that, into something beyond..."[3]

In this chapter it will be our objective to explain what there is about Christianity that is "beyond" all morality.

Defining "morality" and "ethics"

Dictionary definitions indicate that the English word "moral" is etymologically derived from the Latin *moralis*, which is a combination of two other Latin words, *mos* referring to custom, tradition or habit, and *alis* which refers to people. *Moralis* referred to "customs of the people." Present usage of the English words "moral" and "morality" has reference to compliance or conformity with a conception of good or right behavior.

The English word "ethic" is etymologically derived from the Greek word *ethos* that became the root of the Latin word *ethice*. In the *koine* Greek usage of the first century the word *ethos* referred to social custom or habit. Contemporary English usage of "ethic" is essentially synonymous with "morality," referring to the determination of what is good or right and the social approval or disapproval of such activities.

Since the Greek word *ethos*, the root of "ethic," is used on three occasions within the New Testament we will first consider those usages:

(1) Acts 16:21. Paul and Silas are in Philippi. Paul has cast demons out of a young girl who was being used by some men for a fortunetelling venture. The men complain

81

to the magistrates saying, "These men (Paul and Silas)...are proclaiming customs which it is not lawful to accept or observe, being Romans." It is a false accusation that they bring, for Paul was not teaching ethics or morals or customs contrary to Roman law. He was simply proclaiming Jesus Christ.

(2) Acts 26:3. Paul is on trial before King Agrippa at Caeserea. In his defense Paul says, "you (King Agrippa) are an expert in all customs and questions among the Jews." King Agrippa was indeed supposed to be cognizant of the customs and ethics of the Jewish religion. Paul knew that he was not violating God's revelation to the Jews, and was therefore being falsely accused.

(3) I Corinthians 15:33. In the midst of his discussion on the resurrection from the dead, Paul quotes a Greek dramatist, Menander, who had written the motto: "Bad company corrupts good morals." Paul's usage of the quotation is to make the point that sinful behavior will affect what happens in our resurrection from the dead.

So, the three usages of *ethos* in the New Testament are made by: (1) Pandering pimps exploiting a young girl and making a false accusation against Paul. (2) The apostle Paul in a correct observation about Jewish religion. (3) A pagan playwright as an observation about social associations. Not one of these indicates that Christianity has anything to do with morality or ethics.

One other reference in the New Testament where some English translations use the word "moral" should be noted. In II Peter 1:5 the NASB translates, "...in your faith supply moral excellence, and in your moral excellence knowledge." A single Greek word is used for the phrase "moral excellence." The Greek word is *arete*, having to do with virtuous or honorable behavioral expression. The meaning might be an admonition to allow for a consistent behavioral outworking of our faith, but the verse does not advocate morality or ethics as the words are defined and used in the English language today.

"Morality" and "ethics" have to do with human definition and evaluation of human activities, and whether such activities are socially acceptable or unacceptable, approved or unapproved, as right or wrong, good or bad, relative to the intentions and desires of the prevailing human powers and authorities. Although the standard of "moral" determination and "ethical" evaluation may be said to be of God, it is never really any higher than man and his individual or collective attempts to control human behavior.

Determining "good" and "right"

The definitions of "morality" and "ethics" always seem to employ references to good and evil, right and wrong conduct, so it is important to understand how these designations are determined and evaluated. What determines what is "good" or "right"? Do goodness or righteousness exist in and of themselves? Does evil exist in and of itself? Is there such a thing as "autonomous goodness," an autonomous ethic standard, or what Jacques Ellul refers to as the "autonomy of morality?"[4]

Christianity asserts that God alone is autonomous, independent and self-existent. Everything and everyone else is dependent and derivative.

When one posits an autonomous standard of "good" or a separated law of "right" behavior, which is objective to, other than, and outside of God, then such an ideological entity becomes a replacement for God. Such a mental formulation becomes the foundation of social morality as the individuals within that social unit bow down in customary conformity to the ideological idol.

Morality always begins with the premise of autonomy and independent existence. The morality thesis seems to divide into at least three premises:

(1) "Good" exists in itself.
(2) "Good" is knowable in itself.
(3) "Good" is do-able by oneself.

These three premises are antithetical to Christian monotheistic understanding and the gospel of grace. Christianity denies (1) the independent, autonomous self-existent "good;" (2) the self-determined, self-defined, self-discernment of "good" by an alleged independent-self of autonomous man; (3) the self-actuating ability of this alleged independent-self, autonomous man, to generate his own "good" behavior.

There is no "natural goodness" which becomes the basis of a "natural morality" within a "natural theology." "There is none good, no not one" (Rom. 3:12). "No one is good, except God alone" (Luke 18:19). When mankind thinks that he can know "good" and define "good" from his own perspective alone, he ends up calling "evil good, and good evil" (Isa. 5:20), and Isaiah pronounces a woe upon those who are thus "wise in their own eyes, and clever in their own sight" (Isa. 5:21).

The so-called "good" intentions of prevailing moralizers allegedly acting for the "good" of the whole, simply create moralities and ethics based on their fallen and self-serving motivations. They "bind up" others in the tyranny of legalistic performances, encouraging them to strive and struggle to perform goodness, right living, morality, modesty, etc. Such is the bondage of religion and morality.

The Christian gospel, contrary to such religion and morality based on the three premises previously stated, asserts these three monotheistic premises:

(1) "Good" exists only in God.
(2) "Good" is knowable only as God reveals Himself.
(3) "Good" is do-able only as the character of God is activated and expressed in human behavior by the grace of God.

To expand on these premises and document their Biblical basis:

(1) "God is good" is an assertion made throughout the Scriptures. "No one is good except God alone" (Mark 10:18; Luke 18:19). "There is One who is good" (Matt. 19:17). There is no legitimate, genuine, absolute "good" which has any objective, independent, autonomous existence, apart from God. "Good" exists exclusively in the essence of the autonomous God. "Good" can only be defined by the character of God's goodness.

(2) God has revealed Himself, and has thus revealed His character of goodness. "He has told you, O man, what is good" (Micah 6:8). God's telling man what is good is not to be construed merely as a verbalization of a revealed standard of good behavior. God has revealed His goodness in the ultimate revelation of Himself in His Son, Jesus Christ, and that not to be understood as merely historical or theological explanation. We can only really know what good is by knowing God through Jesus Christ. But, again, knowing God and His goodness is not just cerebral, theoretical or academic; such must be living and personal. The revealing of God's goodness and the knowing of God's goodness are not statically contained in an event (incarnation) or an experience (conversion). The knowing of God's goodness is not to be solidified, objectified, or codified in law-form (Law) or in a static written record (Bible), nor formulated and systematized in a static belief-system that becomes "dead letter" (II Cor. 3:6,7; Rom. 2:29). The revealing and the knowing of God's goodness is by an ever-dynamic personal revelation of God as to how He desires to express His goodness in us uniquely and novelly; a new, fresh, spontaneous and living expression of

87

His goodness which can never be contained or explained. God's goodness is knowable only as He reveals Himself.

(3) God's goodness is do-able, expressable in human behavior, only as the character of God is dynamically generated and actuated by God's grace. Only God can actively express His goodness. It is not a commodity to be distributed. It is not a moral pattern to be imitated. God's goodness can be expressed within His creation in human behavior, only by His own energizing, empowering and enabling, i.e. His grace. The active expression of all genuine goodness in our behavior is always derived from God. "The one who does good is of God" (III John 11); "of God" is translated from the Greek phrase *ek theos*, referring to source, origin or derivation from God. In other words, "the one who manifests goodness derives what he does out of God." The expression of goodness in human behavior is always contingent upon God's generating expression of His own character (grace), and the derivative receptivity of God's activity by man (faith). "Good" is do-able only as the character of God is activated in human behavior by the grace of God.

We return now to further document the first premise that "God is good," and that God is the basis of defining all goodness. Alongside the premise that "God is good" one might adduce other premises that assert that something else is "good," whether a person, an object, an idea or an activity. Examples: "Joe is good." "The Bible is good." "Christian belief is good." "Bible reading is good." Can all of these statements be true? Yes. Are they equivalent premises? No. Can anything or anyone else be said to be "good" in the same sense that God is good? No! We must not make ourself, another person, an object, an idea, or an activity equivalent to God.

To apply mathematical logic to these premises, let "God is good" be represented by the equation $x = good$. Anything or anyone else might be represented by $y = good$. If so, then $y = x$, anything else thus represented is equivalent to God; $y = God$. Never! The two premises cannot be maintained as equal premises. To do so is either to deify the person or thing, or to relativize and reduce God to simply an expedient abstraction.

When we state that "God is good," the verb "is" is used in an essential and constitutional sense, but cannot be so used in the other statements. What (Who) God is, only God is! If God is the essence of goodness, then nothing or no one else can be the essence of goodness. This might be referred to as the "non-transferrability of God's attributes." Something or someone else cannot be said to be inherently and essentially what only God exclusively is. We must not attribute an attribute of God to ourselves, another person, an object, an idea, or an activity, for in so doing we deify such and make it an idol.

The Christian assertion that "God is good" is made in reference to His other revealed attributes that may be used adverbially to explain His goodness. God is essentially, inherently, intrinsically, constitutionally, absolutely, perfectly, ultimately, singularly, autonomously, independently, exclusively, supremely, sovereignly, totally, wholly, uniquely, personally, eternally, really good. Thus we clarify and qualify what we mean when we say "God is good." The verb "is" is employed as the third person singular of "to be." God is the being, the essence of all goodness; the reality, the nature of all goodness. God constitutes and comprises goodness. God establishes goodness. These are underlying meanings of our Christian assertion that "God is good."

The verb "to be" has other meanings in the English language, which if thus interpreted in the statement "God is good" would lead to moral and ethical standards contrary to

Christian understanding. When we say, "God is good," we do not mean that God belongs to a class of "goodness" or that God conforms to a "standard of goodness." Nor do we mean that God symbolizes "goodness" or is to be classified, categorized or characterized within a category of "goodness."

What do we mean by the term "good" which forms the object of the statement "God is good"? We can only define and describe "good" by the character of God if He is the source and essence of all good. Thus we employed adverbs to describe good that were but other features of God's character. God's goodness can only be described by His Godliness! The Being of God defines good!

There are other definitions and connotations of "good" in the English language, all of which have a relative evaluation in relation to something else other than God. When we assert that "God is good," we do not mean merely that God is relatively, beneficially, advantageously, profitably, attractively, effectively, suitably, properly, favorably, pleasingly, respectably, honorably, commendably, wholesomely, acceptably, satisfactorily, morally, ethically good. It is not that "God is good" because He conforms to a moral standard, because He provides what is beneficial, because He has utilitarian advantage, because He serves a purpose. If "God is good" because He serves a purpose, then the purpose is higher than God. If "God is good" because He conforms to a moral standard, then the standard is higher than God. God's goodness is thus relative to something else and not absolute in Himself. This would posit an object, idea or activity outside of God, objective to God and by definition superior to God, by which "goodness" is established and determined. It is an idolatrous attribution of an attribute of God to something other than God.

Another subtle mistake is to say that "God is good" because He does good. Divine activity then becomes the objective basis of determining God's character. God's goodness would then be based on His performance. The Psalmist writes, "Thou art good and doest good" (Ps. 119:68). Notice that the statement is not "thou doest good and therefore art good."

God does what He does because He is who He is! His doing springs from His being. His conduct flows out of His character, and He always acts "in character." Christian theology must commence with who God is, not with what God does; not His plan, His purposes, His decrees, His

92

sovereignty, His actions. It is a subtle form of idolatry to allow the conduct of God to supplant and supersede the character of God; the performance of God to be the basis of the Person of God. So much of Western theology has done just that, basing their theology on the purpose and activity of God rather than on the character of God. It is because "God is good" that "God does good." He brings forth His expression out of His good character. It can even be said that He does what He does *ek theos*, out of His own character. He thus activates His own character to be manifested in human behavior. He does what He does, because He is who He is! All good done is done by God, who is good.

When any genuine "goodness" is expressed in the behavior of man, it is the activity of God expressing His character of goodness by His grace. Morality, on the other hand, is based on the thesis of man's self-generated activity conforming to some independent "standard of goodness," which may be identified in some way with God's activity or with social benefit.

When an allegedly independent, autonomous, self-existent ideal of "good" behavioral activity is substituted for God, who alone is independent, autonomous, self-existent "Good," then the ideal has become an idol. The establishment of a standard of good behavioral activities apart from who God is in His character and what God does by His grace, is the establishment of a false substitute for God, i.e. an idol. Any determinative "standard of good" apart from, objective to, or outside of the inherent Being and character of God and the grace activity of God, is necessarily idolatrous!

The humanistic premise of an allegedly independent-self, autonomous man, constructing an allegedly independent, autonomous "standard of good," and then conforming to such by his allegedly independent, autonomous, self-generated, self-activated behavioral activity; that is the foundation on which morality is built. It could not be more antithetical or opposite to Christianity!

Human behavioral activities are not good or evil in themselves (such would be to posit the first premise of moralism) and are not generated by ourselves (such would posit the third premise of moralism). An activity is not inherently good, for only God is inherently good. Human activity is merely "expression." It is not creative generation out of man. We are not gods! We are derivative creatures. Man is not a self-generating actuator of his own activities nor of the character of either good or evil expressed within those activities.

The words "act," "action," and "activity" in the English language are etymologically derived from the Latin words *actus*, "doing," and *actum*, "thing done." Human activity is always enacted by an actuator. A spiritual personage is the agent of activation, causing and moving a particular character to be activated and expressed in our behavior. Our behavior and the character expressed therein is always enacted (in-acted), caused to be activated within. It is not self-generated, auto-creative, activated by the self-effort of human effort. There is always a derivative contingency to human behavior. All that we do is contingent on the spiritual action of a spiritual being allowed by our decision-making to act out in our behavior. The spiritual being who empowers, enables, energizes and enacts our behavioral expression always conveys his particular character in the activity; character of either good or evil, out of either God or Satan. The character that is being expressed in any human activity must be traced back to its spiritually empowering actuator. Human behavior always expresses the character of the energizing spirit who is the actuator of that expression being enacted in human behavior. For example, Jesus observed the religious and moral external activities of the Pharisees and concluded that there was a spiritual empowering actuator behind what they did: "You are of your father, the devil..." (John 8:44).

Mankind always has a derived spiritual condition, based on the spiritual indwelling of a spiritual being, and a derived behavior expression, manifesting the character of the spiritual being who is energizing (*energeo*, to work in) and enacting (*en-actus*, to do in) the human activity.

Whenever we might refer to a man being good, it is never in the same sense that "God is good." Man is not essentially good, constitutionally good, inherently good or intrinsically good. Man is not by nature good; neither does he establish goodness; nor is he self-generatively good. A man's goodness is relative to his deriving the expression of God's character of goodness in his spiritual condition and in his behavioral expression.

Consistent reasoning must apply this to the opposite expression also, in the realm of theodicy. God is good. The Evil One is evil. Man is evil, not in the same sense that the Evil one is evil. Man is not essentially evil, constitutionally evil, inherently evil, intrinsically evil. Man is not by nature evil; does not establish evil; is not definitively evil; is not

self-generatively evil. Man is not a devil. A man is evil
only relative to his deriving the expression of the character
of the Evil One in his spiritual condition and behavioral
expression.

The point being made is that there is a derivative
determination of good and evil from the nature and
character of God and Satan, respectively. There is no
autonomous good or evil (first premise of moralism). There
is no self-determined awareness of good or evil (second
premise of moralism). There is no humanly generated good
or evil (third premise of moralism).

The historical origins of this derivative character
expression in man must be traced back to the Biblical
account in Genesis two and three. It is there that we
discover the first fallacious attempts of man to determine
good and evil autonomously, apart from their
consubstantiality in God or Satan.

The "tree of life" represented the choice of man to
recognize that goodness exists in God alone (first theistic
premise), that good was knowable only by listening to
God's revelation (second theistic premise), and that by
volitional receptivity to God's indwelling provision of His
Life there was divine sufficiency to manifest the character

of God's goodness in man's behavior (third theistic premise). Thus man was free to function as God intended by the expression of the character of the Creator within the behavior of the creature; free to be and do what God intended to be and do in man.

The "tree of the knowledge of good and evil," on the other hand, was a rejection of God's intent. The "father of lies" (John 8:44) wanted to "cover-up" the derivative determination of good and evil. He foisted upon man the delusional idea of self-determined morality, that man could be "like God, knowing good and evil" (Gen. 3:5), establishing and determining good and evil by oneself, independent, from one's own perspective and center of reference.

> "Satan persuaded man...that he had an adequate capacity in himself for being good, without the necessity of having God; that he could be righteous in his own right, morally adult without the need of being spiritually alive! In short, that man could be independent -- both cause and effect!"[5]

That is where morality started, at the fall of man. Thenceforth man was naturally self-deceived with respect to his ability to be the arbiter and generator of good and evil, thinking that he could establish ethical standards of good and evil, right and wrong, on the basis of human self-evaluation of individual and collective social "good." Natural man has posited the three premises of moralism ever since: (1) self-existent good, (2) self-determined good, (3) self-potential of good. The moralities of men, with their relativized, self-oriented standards of good and evil, are always contrary to God's intent, always sinful, and always derived from satanic source.

The Rejection of Morality

Morality is antithetical to all Christian belief and behavior. Admittedly, if one does not understand the foundation already laid in differentiating between morality and Christianity, and the derivation of good and evil from God or Satan respectively, then the statements below will appear to be bizarre, outlandish and almost blasphemous.

(1) Morality is a joke. It is a bad joke that is not even funny, because it is tragic. For the dedicated religionist, morality is no joking matter. It is the basis of his religion. But for the Christian, morality is a joke.

It was C.S. Lewis who first expressed this thought.

"I think all Christians would agree with me if I said that though Christianity seems at first to be all about morality, all about duties and rules and guilt and virtue, yet it leads you on, out of all that, into something beyond. One has a glimpse of a country where they do not talk of these things, except perhaps as a joke. Everyone there is filled full with what we should call goodness as a mirror is filled with light. But they do not call it goodness. They do not call it anything. They are not thinking of it. They are too busy looking at the source from which it comes."[6]

Has anyone ever become "good" or "righteous" on the basis of morally proper behavior? Impossible! Absurd! That is what makes morality such a laughable matter: its utter absurdity and impossibility (the basis of many a joke). Morality is Satan's big laugh on mankind.

(2) Morality is a result of the fall of man into sin. As noted, the deceptive temptation of the Tempter in the garden of Eden was to suggest that man could develop a self-determined knowledge of good and evil. That was the first temptation – to develop morality, to establish an independent, self-oriented standard of good and evil. Rejecting the derived goodness of God, man opted for the lie. Natural men, religious men, have been developing moralities ever since, trying to regulate man's behavior.

(3) Morality is a lie. It is based on the lie of independent-self, autonomous man. The true condition of man is that of derivative contingency upon spiritual being for both spiritual condition and behavioral expression.

(4) Morality is sinful. If sin is defined as anything not derived from God, then morality is sinful because it

100

advocates the autonomy of goodness and fails to understand the spiritual derivativeness of all human behavior. "Whatever is not of faith is sin" (Rom. 14:23), and morality is not based on the derived receptivity of faith. Therefore it is sinful.

(5) Morality is humanistic. Humanism is based on the thesis of the autonomous self-potential of mankind, the suggestion of which was first introduced in the garden. Morality is humanistic because "goodness" is alleged to be knowable by oneself (second premise of moralism) and do-able by oneself (third premise of moralism). The self-potential of self-generated, self-activated behavioral activity is at the root of all morality.

(6) Morality is psychological manipulation. Behavioristic psychology attempts to manipulate human behavior in "behavior modification," failing to understand the spiritual source of all behavior. The social moralists employ such behavioristic psychological manipulation to keep their particular "society" or social unit in check and functioning in accord with their self-oriented objectives.

(7) Morality is offensive to God. God hates morality! It is contrary to His intent for mankind. Isaiah graphically states that "all our righteous deeds are as a filthy rag"

101

(Isaiah 64:6). All our moral actions by which we try to be good or righteous, when presented before God are as offensive as presenting Him with a menstrual cloth, a "dirty Kotex!" (This is the literal meaning of the Hebrew words.) Lest you be offended at such graphic analogy, just be aware that God is even more offended at our periodic discharges of morality – presentations which are the discharge of death with no life.

The picture is no prettier when Paul describes his religious and moral efforts as but "rubbish" or "dung" (KJV) in Philippians 3:8. One preacher put Paul's statement in contemporary vernacular by declaring that "self-righteous morality is nothing but a pile of shit." Morality is offensive to God.

(8) Morality is "another gospel." When Paul wrote to the Galatians warning them of the religionists who were trying to add moralistic requirements to the simple gospel of grace in Jesus Christ, he indicated that they were bringing "another gospel" which was "no gospel" at all since it was devoid of any "good news." History is replete with moral supplements becoming part and parcel of so-called "Christian religion." Whenever morality is

introduced it supplants the singular sufficiency of Jesus Christ and constitutes "another gospel."

(9) Morality is "salvation by works." Morality posits activity that is supposedly derived from oneself, and is therefore "salvation by works." Paul wrote to the Ephesians explaining, "For by grace are you saved through faith, that not of yourselves, it is the gift of God, not of works lest any man should boast" (Eph. 2:8,9). Salvation is always enacted by the dynamic of God's saving work in the provision of His grace. The commencement of that salvation is in conversion, but the continuing dynamic of the "saving life" of Jesus Christ (Rom. 5:10) makes us safe from satanic misuse, abuse and dysfunction in order to restore us to the functional use God intended by His grace activity in the Christian.

(10) Morality is legalism. Morality sets up a "standard" of behavior, a codification of acceptable conduct. These rules and regulations of right and wrong form an independent, external law, to which all subjects are expected to conform. Striving to conform to the law is thus the moralistic objective of "obedience." Moralistic, legalistic "obedience to the law" is far removed from the

"obedience of faith" (Rom. 1:5) that listens under God's Spirit and is obedient to Life.

(11) Morality is deadly. There is certainly no vibrancy and vitality of divine life in the legalism of morality. Paul writes in II Cor. 3:6, "the letter kills, but the Spirit gives life." The "letter of the law" on which morality rests is deadly! It kills all expression of God's life in man, as man works himself to death!

(12) Morality is devastating and destructive. Incapable of ever measuring up to the moral requirements, man is increasingly frustrated, unhappy and grieved. James S. Stewart, the Scottish preacher, writes,

> "The evangel of an ethical example is a devastating thing. It makes religion the most grievous of burdens. Perhaps this is the reason why, even among professing Christians, there are so many strained faces and weary hearts and captive, unreleased spirits."[7]

In addition, we might add that the morality that is inherent in religion is a most maddening experience; it drives a person "mad."

(13) Morality is bondage. Morality binds a person up, making them slaves to law, convention and social approval. To the Galatians Paul explained, "It was for freedom that Christ set us free;...do not be subject again to a yoke of slavery" (Gal. 5:1). Morality destroys the freedom to be and

do whatever God wants to be and do in us. The rigid chains of moral inflexibility allow for no novelty, newness, no spontaneity of fresh expression of the Spirit.

(14) Morality is Pharisaical. The Pharisees engaged in their perpetual pretense of piety. Though their moralistic attempts are often called "self-righteousness," in reality they had a pseudo-righteousness, no righteousness at all, just sin! Jesus detested, opposed and exposed the Pharisaical morality. Frank Lake recognized the Pharisaism of morality:

> "Ethical behavior by itself can too easily entrench a man in self-righteousness. He has joined the Pharisee, praying with himself to a god who is not the Father of our Lord Jesus Christ, 'I thank thee that I am not as other men are.' ...No mortal man can win by self-effort what in the nature of things must always be a gift."[8]

(15) Morality is fraudulent. It can never deliver what it promises. It does not achieve the results it is designed to achieve. Paul explains in Colossians 2:23 that morality is of "no value against fleshly indulgence." The patterned propensities of selfishness and sinfulness in the desires of our soul will never be dealt with, or overcome by, moral suppressionism or by moral striving to overcome.

(16) Morality is a contrived substitute for Christian living. As a posturing pretext of living a "good Christian

life," morality plays the part of an impostor. Jacques Ellul notes that

> "morality is the means whereby the Christian dodges death in Christ and fashions a living way of his own. It is the worst of all illusions."[9]

Instead of disallowing our selfish expressions by allowing the life of Jesus Christ to be lived out through us, morality masquerades self-oriented conformity as "spiritual behavior." Hypocrisy!

(17) Morality is idolatry. Ian Thomas writes of

> "seeking to be godly by submitting yourself to external rules and regulations, and by conformity to behavior patterns imposed upon you by the particular Christian society which you have chose, and in which you hope to be found 'acceptable.' You will in this way perpetuate the pagan habit of practicing religion in the energy of the 'flesh,' and in the very pursuit of righteousness commit idolatry in honoring 'Christianity' more than Christ."[10]

Morality reduces God to a "thing," a moral ideal, an ethical standard, a religious expectation of conformity and a behavioral formula. The ideal becomes an ideological idol constructed and carved in the human mind. The religious moralist then submits to the moral ideal, rather than to God.

(18) Morality is satanic. Despite the fact that many religious people equate morality with godliness, it is really

the deceptive and diabolic tactic of the deceiver. The devil, the "father of lies" (John 8:44) and all falsehood, has substituted a fallacious system of behavioral guidelines as the basis of "goodness." The "god of this world" (II Cor. 4:4) has blinded the minds of men to keep them from seeing that anything not derived from God is evil and sinful. In the name of "religion," morality calls the selfishly motivated efforts of man "good" and "righteous," when they are but evil derived from the Evil One.

(19) Morality is a religious inevitability. Wherever you find religion you will find morality? They are always "coupled" together. Why? Because religion is a man-made, Satan-inspired, social organization that requires morality standards to give it external form, to give it *raison d'etre*, to cement loyalty and conformity, and to keep the guilt payments coming in. As people perceive their inability to please and appease God by their inadequate moral behavior, they seek to buy off their sin in "indulgences."

(20) Morality is a worldly necessity. In the society of the "world," that is of fallen mankind, morality is necessitated to keep the chaos of selfishness and sinfulness "in check," if even temporarily. Again Jacques Ellul writes that morality

"is part of the condition of the fall. Now endowed with the power to define good and evil, to elaborate it, to know it and to pretend to obey it, man can no longer renounce this power that he has purchased so dearly. He cannot live without morality."[11]

The worldliness of human society, fallen man in this fallen world, necessitates morality. Morality is of the order of worldliness!

(21) Morality is relative. Human, social, worldly and religious morality is never properly related to the absoluteness of God's character of goodness, and to the absolutely only expression of God's goodness by derivation from God by God's grace. Morality is relative to the intents and desires of the prevailing authorities in the particular society over which they have manipulative control (ex. governmental, ecclesiastical, etc.) Morality is relative to the majority of the individuals in that society willing to accept the moral standards, either under threat of punishment or by democratic consensus of what is "good" and/or "evil" with an individual accountability to the so-called "good" of the whole. Morality is relative to the limitations of fallen man in keeping such moral conditions, due to the patterned selfishness and sinfulness of the "flesh."

(22) Morality is antithetical to Christianity. Morality always attempts to establish "goodness" apart from its

derivation out of God alone, and its availability to man by the indwelling of Jesus Christ alone. Morality denies the derived existence of good in the character of God. Morality denies the derived knowledge of good by the revelation of God. Morality denies the derived expression of good by the grace of God. Morality precludes the primary assertion of the Christian gospel, that the availability for the expression of God's goodness in man is only by the presence and empowering of the Spirit of Christ in man, received by faith in regeneration and sanctification.

Morality never creates Christian behavior. Once again Ellul remarks that

> "Morality...necessarily collides with God's decision brought to pass in Jesus Christ, which locates the life and truth of man out beyond anything that man can formulate, know and live."[12]

> Christianity is "antimorality."[13]

The Distinctive of Christianity and Christian behavior

What has already been noted by contrast must now be explained more explicitly: the radical difference of the Christian gospel from all moralities. C.S. Lewis expresses this so succinctly when he writes that Christianity

> "differs from ordinary ideas of 'morality' and 'being good.' ...the whole of Christianity is 'putting on Christ.' Christianity offers nothing else."[14]

Then elsewhere he writes,

"...the Christian is in a different position from other people who are trying to be good. ...the Christian thinks that any good he does comes from the Christ-life inside him."[15]

Having previously noted that "God is good," and that this statement is semantically and philosophically different than any other statement that refers to goodness, the distinctive of Christianity begins with the fact that Jesus Christ is God and therefore Jesus Christ is good. Jesus as God is the essence of goodness, by nature good, absolutely good, independently good, the source of all good in the Christian.

The monotheistic premises noted previously were (1) Good exists only in God. (2) Good is knowable only as God reveals His character. (3) Good is do-able only as the character of God is expressed by the grace of God. In the Christian assertion that Jesus Christ is God the premises concerning goodness are defined even more distinctively. Every Christian has "in Jesus Christ" (1) the presence of the good within him/her by the indwelling presence of Jesus Christ, (2) the on-going revelation of the good by the active enlightenment of the Spirit of Christ, (3) the capability of expressing God's character of goodness by the energizing, enabling and empowering of the Spirit of Christ. The

Christian has received the presence of God, the life of Jesus Christ, within his/her spirit at regeneration, constituting the restoration of God's intent for His human creation. Any connection of God's goodness to man's spiritual condition or behavioral expression is only by the spiritual reception of the life of Jesus Christ by faith. Jesus said, "No man cometh unto the Father, but by Me" (John 14:6). We might adapt that to read, "No man cometh unto Goodness, but by Me."

Some clarifications need to be made at the outset as we consider how God's goodness is connected to the Christian:

When we become Christians and receive the Good-One, the God-One, Jesus Christ, into our spirit, this is not to imply that we become good, and now are good, for we have already asserted that only "God is good." Scripture does indicate that the Roman Christians were "full of goodness" (Rom. 15:14); that Christians are "made perfect" (Heb. 12:23); and that we "become the righteousness of God in Him" (II Cor. 5:21). But to indicate that we are made, that we become, that we are good, perfect, righteous, holy etc. must be done within the context of the presence of God in Christ. When reference is made to becoming good, being made good, righteous or holy, this is never to say that we are good inherently, intrinsically, independently, autonomously, or eternally. We have received the Good-One, the God-One, Jesus, into the core of our being, into our spirit. We are thus identified with the Good-One, and in terms of our spiritual identity we might be known as "good ones," "God-ones," "godly," "righteous ones," "justified," "holy ones," "saints," "sanctified," "Christ-ones," "Christians." Such designations are only and always based on the indwelling presence of Jesus Christ, never on any alleged reality that has become intrinsic within and unto ourselves. "The container never becomes the contents." To quote Jacques Ellul again,

"The entire Bible constantly iterates that nothing has changed intrinsically or ontologically in this person who has been enlightened by the revelation. He is saved. He is justified. He is sanctified, but he is still himself."[16]

In other words, the Christian is still a derivative man, deriving both spiritual condition and behavioral expression from the spiritual source of Jesus Christ. We must avoid all forms of perfectionism that might imply that we are perfect, good, holy or righteousness essentially, constitutionally and/or inherently.

Whereas the first clarification has to do with a denial of lapsing back into the first premise of moralism, the second clarification concerns itself with a denial of lapsing into the second and third premises of moralism.

When we become Christians and receive the Good-One, the God-One, Jesus Christ, into our spirit, this is not to imply that we have now been invested with the inherent ability to know what is good, or the inherent capability to do the good. Ellul explains that the Christian does not have

"any intrinsic capacity to do by himself the good which God has set forth. There is no permanent transformation of his being which would consist in this ability to perform the will of God by Himself."[17]

This is precisely where so much of the teaching of Christian religion has jumped track into the second and third premises of moralism. For centuries the gospel has been typically presented as the Good-One, the God-One, Jesus Christ being incarnated as a man, and living out the good-life perfectly, "without sin" (Heb. 4:15; II Cor. 5:21). Accurate history. Accurate theology. What usually happens then is that the historic "presentation" of perfect goodness in human behavior in the life of Jesus Christ on earth is made to be the "standard" to which those who assent to, or receive, Jesus Christ are expected to look to in order to know good (second premise) and conform to in order to do good (third premise). Such is the tragic "sell-out" of the

113

Christian gospel "down the river" into mere morality! Christian religion has taught *The Imitation of Christ* (Thomas A'Kempis) by walking *In His Steps* (Charles Sheldon) in order to be *Like Christ* (Andrew Murray).

Paul's explanation of Christian behavior is that of "the manifestation of the life of Jesus in our mortal bodies" (II Cor. 4:10,11); not by any human imitation of Christ's behavioral goodness. Christian living is not "monkey see, monkey do," the parroting or aping of reproduced external behavior. The distinctive of Christian behavior is that the life of Jesus Christ is lived out in our behavior, the character of God's goodness manifested in our behavior. "It is no longer I who lives, but Christ lives in me, and the life that I now live in the flesh, I live by faith in the Son of God, who loved me and gave Himself up for me" (Gal. 2:20). The expression of behavioral goodness is not by any capability or effort from within man. Jesus said, "Apart from Me, you can do nothing" (John 15:5). Apart from Jesus, we can do nothing that manifests the character of God. Apart from Jesus, we can do nothing good. Apart from Jesus, we can do nothing that glorifies God. Apart from Jesus, we can do nothing that qualifies as Christian behavior.

Thus we proceed to further amplify that Jesus Christ is the sole source of all good behavior in the Christian. Jesus is the sole source of the knowledge of good behavior. Jesus is the sole source of the enacting of good behavior, being the expression of God's character of goodness.

Goodness is known and activated only by God's grace. Grace is "God's activity consistent with His character."

The only way we can know the goodness of God, in the awareness of His attributes and character, and in the knowledge of how God in Christ wishes to express His goodness in our behavior, is that by His grace God reveals Himself and His intent to us. It is one thing to know that God is good intellectually, even based on Biblical information and history, but it is another thing to know that God is good personally and experientially, and to know how He desires to express that goodness through man. We know the intent of God in expressing His goodness through us only by the grace of God whereby the Spirit of Christ continues to reveal, to enlighten and to illumine our spiritual understanding. We "listen under" His instruction in the "obedience of faith" in order to know how, when, where and to whom He wishes to manifest His goodness through us. This gracious personal revelation of His goodness in and through us as Christian is ever-new, novel, unique, fresh and spontaneous. It cannot be explained in ecclesiastical rules and regulations. It cannot be contained in codifications of conduct. It cannot be retained and restrained in repetitive rituals. It cannot be objectified into Biblical blueprints. It cannot be made static. God's expressions of goodness cannot be put in a box! God will reveal (Phil. 3:15) His goodness so that we might know His goodness and how it is that He desires to express His goodness in our behavior by His grace.

Likewise, the distinctive of the Christian gospel for the doing of goodness, the manifestation of goodness, is only and always the activity of God by the indwelling presence of the Spirit of Christ. "God is at work in you both to will and to work for His good pleasure" (Phil. 2:13). God is energizing both the motivation and the out-working of our behavior in accord with His good character and for His good pleasure, unto His glory. God in Christ will do what He desires, and He will do so by the dynamic of His own self-generated expression of goodness. III John 11 reads, "The one doing good is of God." As previously noted, "of God" is *ek theos* in Greek, meaning "out of God." Any time we manifest genuine goodness it is derived out of the character of God, expressed and enacted by the power and grace of God.

Whenever we come across the New Testament admonitions exhorting us to "know good" and to "do good," we must always remember that the dynamic for doing so is in God, in Christ.

Romans 16:19 - "I want you to be wise in what is good." How? By allowing God to continue to reveal His goodness.

Gal. 6:9,10 - "let us not lose heart in doing good...let us do good to all men." How? By the dynamic of God's doing of His goodness in and through us.

I Thess. 5:21 - "hold fast to what is good; abstain from every form of evil." What is good? That which expresses God's character of goodness. How are we going to hold fast to that and abstain from every form of evil? Three verses later in I Thess 5:24 we read, "Faithful is He who calls you, He also will bring it to pass."

II Thess. 3:13 - "do not grow weary of doing good." What is to weary us if we recognize that it is not our struggling and striving to perform goodness? It is possible to grow weary of the fact that so few seem to recognize and appreciate that it is God's goodness expressed in our behavior.

As Christians we are to continue to be available and receptive in faith to the expression of God's goodness in our behavior. "He who began a good work in you, will perfect it until the day of Christ Jesus" (Phil. 1:6). The "good work" that God intends will not be perfected by our conforming to a "standard of goodness," nor by our generating, manufacturing, mustering up good behavior (were we able to do so), but only by the dynamic of divine grace, and our receptivity of that activity in faith.

Jesus allows us the freedom to express His goodness in our behavior. Such expression is not forced upon the Christian. As Christians we still have freedom of choice. We are still choosing creatures. Even though Eph. 2:10 states that "we are created in Christ Jesus for good works, which God prepared beforehand that we should walk in them," this does not necessarily imply that all our behavioral expressions are predetermined in a rigid, closed-system, thus denying freedom of choice.

In Jesus Christ we have freedom unto the intended function of our humanity. We are free to be and do all that God wants to be and do in us. The intention of the Creator

God was to dwell within, and activate His character of goodness through the creature man. By the fall of mankind into sin, and their spiritual enslavement to the Evil One (II Tim. 2:26), they became "slaves of sin" and to the expression of his character of evil. In Jesus Christ we are restored to God's intent by God's indwelling and dynamic activity in us. Free to be man as God intended man to be, by the presence and power of Jesus Christ in us. Freedom is a most important concept of Christianity. Jesus said, "You shall know the Truth, and the Truth shall set you free" (John 8:32), and then, "If therefore the Son shall make you free, you shall be free indeed" (John 8:36). Paul explained, "It was for freedom that Christ set us free...do not be subject again to a yoke of slavery" (Gal. 5:1); "You were called to freedom, brethren" (Gal. 5:13). "Where the spirit of the Lord is, there is liberty" (II Cor. 3:17). We are free to be good as God intended man to be. Free to love God and allow His goodness to be expressed through us for others. What freedom! Augustine explained that we can "love God and do what we want."

The religionist only understands freedom as freedom *from* something rather than freedom *to* God's intent. He seems only to conceive of freedom in the context of law,

119

rather than freedom of function. So there is nothing that frightens the religionist or moralist more than freedom from the legal standards of good behavior that have been posited in place of God. They reason, "If man is free from the law, free from moral codes, free from the religious manipulation thereof, there is no telling what man might do. It would be chaos!" It is thereby revealed that they have not taken God into account. They only understand "goodness" in the idolatrous context of conformity to behavioral law codes.

When the apostle Paul shared the gospel of grace, the freedom that we have in Jesus Christ, the religious critics, the Judaizers, indicated that he was advocating antinomianism, that he was teaching "against the law," that he was encouraging lawlessness, licentiousness, libertinism. Paul wrote in Rom. 6:15, "Shall we sin because we are not under the law but under grace? May it never be!" (cf. Rom. 3:5,8; 6:1). Freedom to sin is a total misunderstanding of grace and freedom.

Freedom in Christ is indeed on the far side of moralistic legalism. From the confined and false perspective of legalism such freedom will appear to be lawlessness, violations of regulatory behavioral law and moral standards of goodness. But the Law of God has as its primary

120

function the revelation of the character of God, and grace is the divine dynamic to express that character of God freely in the Christian.

Jesus Christ wants to express His character of goodness in consistent, practical Christian behavior. The message of the Christian gospel is not just ethereal theory about abstract "goodness," or philosophizing and theologizing about "goodness." We do not want to be so heavenly-minded that we are of no earthly good. Christian living has to do with practical behavior that consistently expresses the character of God. Christian living has to do with the practicalities of God's goodness being expressed in all of our interpersonal relationships; husbands and wives, parents and children, employers and employees, friends, acquaintances and general public.

Paul warns us "do not turn your freedom into an opportunity for the flesh" (Gal. 5:13). There have been libertarian advocates who have so reacted to moralism, as to eschew and repudiate all behavioral considerations and preaching. They are willing to tolerate any behavior in the name of "freedom." We are seeing an epidemic of such tolerance in our society today. It may be a valid backlash against moralism, but it leads to social chaos apart from the recognition of God's grace-expression of goodness.

Sin is still sin! It is not derived from God. It does not express the character of God. It is instead derived from the devil (I John 3:8) and expresses the character of the Evil One.

Whenever the Christian misrepresents the character of God in his behavior by infidelity, dishonesty, greed, strife, jealousy, anger, dissensions, drunkenness, etc. then the intent of God to express His character in that Christian is not taking place. It is a tragic misrepresentation of the life of Jesus Christ.

As we allow the Christ-life to be lived out in our behavior, manifesting God's goodness by His grace, we conversely disallow the "fleshly indulgences" (Col. 2:23), which religious moralism was impotent to deal with. We disallow fleshliness to be selfishly, sinfully and satanically expressed in our behavior. Thus it is that we "deny ourselves" (Luke 9:23) and "abstain from every form of evil" (I Thess 5:22). As we allow Christ to manifest His good-life in our behavior, He thus supersedes, overcomes and disallows the misrepresentative sinful behavior expressions. The positive swallows up the negative.

Jesus Christ wants to express His character of goodness in the social community of the Church. The Church is the "Body of Christ" intended to collectively express the character of Christ. The Church is the "People of God" expressing the character of God's goodness. Paul writes, "Let us do good to all men, and especially to those who are of the household of faith" (Gal. 6:10). There is particular emphasis on God's goodness being expressed in the context of the Church, for it is there that God wants to demonstrate the interpersonal social community that He intended for man as they allow the Creator to function within His creatures. In the Church God wants to show that man can dwell together with man in "peace," when they allow God's goodness to be expressed one to another. The Church is to be the one place that demonstrates how God's people can get along with one another in goodness when each person is receptive to God's love and goodness being expressed to the other, despite diversity of race, sex, age, nationality, intelligence, personality type, difference of opinions, etc.

The distinctive of Christianity and Christian behavior is the awareness that all goodness is derived from God in personal relationship with Jesus Christ, and that all goodness is behaviorally expressed by the dynamic of

123

God's grace alone, which is the out-working of Christ's life. The God who is good is the actuator who activates the expression of His good character and enacts (in-acts) His good character in Christian behavior. God in Christ enables, empowers, energizes and enacts all good behavior, all Christian behavior.

Behavioral goodness is a fruit of the Spirit of Christ. "The fruit of the Spirit is love, joy, peace, patience, kindness, goodness..."(Gal. 5:22,23). "The fruit of the Light consists in all goodness..."(Eph. 5:9). "We walk in a manner worthy of the Lord, to please Him in all respects, bearing fruit in every good work..."(Col. 1:10). It is not that we produce or manufacture goodness or perform goodness, but we bear the fruit of goodness derived from the dynamic of God's divine character. Jesus says, "I am the vine; you are the branches; he who abides in Me and I in him, he bears much fruit; for apart from Me you can do nothing" (John 15:5).

Our focus must be on the divine source of all goodness. Our focus must be on Jesus Christ. "We fix our eyes on Jesus" (Heb. 12:2). Our theology, our lives, must be Christocentric; not morality-centered, not even good-centered, but God-centered, Christ-centered. Returning to the quotation of C.S. Lewis,

> "Christianity leads you on, out of morality, into something beyond. One has a glimpse of a country where they do not talk of those things, except perhaps as a joke. Every one there is filled full with what we shall call goodness as a mirror is filled with light. But they do not call it goodness. They do not call it anything. They are not thinking of it. They are too busy looking at the source from which it comes."[18]

The distinctive of Christianity and Christian behavior is that Christians are looking only at the source of all things in Christ and deriving all from Him by the dynamic of His grace.

An Historical Survey of the Failure to Differentiate Christian Behavior and Morality

Beginning at the beginning of all history, we recall again the intent of God in His creation, which was to be the constantly creative dynamic within His creature, man, in order to manifest His divine character by His divine grace unto His own glory. "We were created for His glory" (Isa. 43:7). It takes God in a man for man to be man as God intended man to be. By man's receptivity to God's life in the "tree of life," God's goodness would have been

125

expressed in man's behavior, the character of the invisible God made visible, imaged in man.

In the fall of man into sin, Adam rejected that derivative relationship of grace/faith, and chose instead the deceiving lie that he could be "like God," an independent, autonomous self, and develop for himself a self-determined standard of "good and evil." Such was the establishment of humanism, morality and religion. Ever since the Fall man has had to exercise the right he demanded, and has had to devise and develop religion in order to fabricate a morality wherewith to stabilize the chaos of his society and attempt to draw man's attention away from himself, if even temporarily, for the good of the whole. "Morality is of the order of the fall."[19]

After the Fall, we observe in the historical narratives of the Old Testament that God begins to paint preliminary "pictures" of how He will remedy man's predicament and restore Himself to man. God picked the Jews to be His "picture" people. He gave them the Law, inclusive of the Ten Commandments, on Mt. Sinai. Judaism was a religion, complete with morality, as all religion is. God established the religion of Judaism to demonstrate the bankruptcy of all religion, and the inability of man to keep any morality, i.e.

to show man that he did not have what it took to be man as God intended.

What about the Old Testament Law? Does it have any reference to Christian behavior? The Law had more than one purpose, and the failure to understand this will lead to many interpretive problems. (1) The essential purpose of the Law was the revelation of the character of God. God is singular, personal, exclusive, worthy of worship. God is faithful, true, needs nothing, etc. (2) The instrumental purpose of the Law was to provide a means with which to reveal the impotence of morality and to evidence the inability of natural, fallen, sinful man to express the character of God, the purpose for which he was created.

After he became a Christian, Paul could still say, "The Law is good, holy, righteous" (Rom. 7:12,13). As we have noted that only "God is good," it is safe to say that Paul did not mean that the "Law is good" in the same sense that "God is good," for he would never have idolatrously equated the Law with God. Rather, the Law is beneficially good; the law serves the good purpose of God, primarily to reveal God's character. Paul makes it very clear elsewhere that the Law does not make anyone good or righteous. "Israel, pursuing a law of righteousness, did not arrive at

127

that law...because they did not pursue it by faith" (Rom. 9:31). "...not knowing about God's righteousness, and seeking to establish their own, they did not subject themselves to the righteousness of God" (Rom. 10:3). "Man is not made righteous by the works of the Law.." (Gal. 2:16). Paul denies that the Law, functionally and religiously employed as a morality, could ever effect God's intent to express His goodness and righteousness and holiness in man's behavior. The "letter kills" Paul wrote (II Cor. 3:6). However, the rabbinic moralists of the Jewish religion continued to carefully craft definitions of precise performance for every eventuality in the legalistic minutia of the Talmudic Mishnah. Judeo-Christian religion today still calculates the moralistic regulatory purpose of the Law.

Outside of the Hebrew context, the philosophers of the world attempted to develop and dictate moralities for mankind. The oriental philosophers such as Buddha, Lao Tzu and Confucius, as well as Greek philosophers such as Socrates, Plato and Aristotle, engaged in this process. All of them, in their own way, attempted to classify moralistic virtues in self-determined categories of good and evil,

128

failing to understand the divine intent of man's deriving all character expression from God.

"In the fullness of time God sent forth His Son" (Gal. 4:4), incarnated as a man in order to take the death consequences of mankind upon Himself, and that in order to restore the life of God to man, so that man could function as God intended. The death of Jesus Christ on the cross was the vindication of all goodness and grace over sin and death. The resurrection of Jesus was the manifestation of the availability of all goodness and grace in the dynamic of the life of the risen Lord Jesus. The "good news" of the gospel is that in Jesus Christ we have the restoration of God's presence and function in man which was lost in the fall. The divine dynamic is restored to man so that all might be derived from God; the Spirit of Christ living and functioning in the Christian.

The grace and freedom made available in Jesus Christ is a radical contradiction to all legalistic morality; to all religion! Most of the New Testament is an exposé of religion; an explanation of the dichotomous difference of Christianity from all religion, especially from the religion of Judaism. Throughout the gospels Jesus exposes and disposes the Pharisees. His parables are poignant pictorial parodies of the religious premises and practices of Pharisaical Judaism. The book of Acts is an historical narrative of nascent Christianity breaking free from the religion of Judaism. Paul's letter to the Romans explains that righteousness is not in religion, but only in Christ. The letter to the Galatians explains the dichotomy of the gospel and religion. The letter to the Hebrews explains that the new covenant in Christ forever obsoletes and abrogates the old covenant of Jewish religion. So it is with every other book of the New Testament.

The grace of God operative in the Christian, the freedom to be and do all God wants to be and do in us; these are opposed to "law" and "works." The moralistic regulatory function of the Law is forever dissipated, destroyed, dispensed with, discarded, and damned!

Despite this gloriously liberating reality of the Christian gospel, the natural, religious man does not like "grace" and "freedom;" it takes away all his "control." So even within the context of the first century, the reaction of the religionists, the moralists, is recorded in the New Testament itself. The Judaizers seemed to follow Paul wherever he went, attempting to impose religious morality on the new Christians, attempting to supplement the gospel of grace with external morality strictures. They wanted to keep a legalistic law-based morality; the very thing Jesus had come to put an end to by His grace! Paul would have none of it. He indicated that what they were teaching was "another gospel" which was "not gospel at all." It was damnable! (Gal.1:6-10).

Within the second and third centuries A.D. we look back to the writings of the early Church fathers, also called the Apostolic Fathers, the earliest extant writings of Christians after the New Testament writings. We search their writings to determine what perspective they had of the gospel of grace, and the freedom of the Christian "in Christ." Did they retain Paul's understanding of the dynamic of Christ's life functioning in the Christian? Regrettably, they did not! Their primary concern seems to have been moralistic conformity, emphasizing external conduct rather than the internal spiritual dynamic of God's grace. T.F. Torrance reports,

> "What occupied the foreground of their (Apostolic fathers) thought was how they were going to walk in the way of this life, and conform to its high standards. So concerned were they about right and wrong behaviour that everywhere they were driven into legalism and formalism. The Christian ethic was codified, and the charismatic life under the constraining love of Christ reduced to rules and precepts. Law and obedience, reward and punishment, these were the themes of their preaching. The centre of gravity was

shifted from the mainspring of the Christian life in the person of Christ Himself to the periphery of outward conformity and daily behaviour."[20]

By the second and third centuries there was developing a "Christian religion" contrary to the Christian gospel. Many of the advocates of early Christian morality systems were labeled as "heretics" – their morality emphases were part of serious theological errors that were condemned. They were trying to integrate Greek philosophy and Gnosticism with the gospel. They were advocating moralistic asceticism as the antidote for "fleshly indulgence." It does not work! (Col. 2:23)

Early in the fourth century, by about 325 A.D., the church became integrated with the state, as Constantine declared Christianity the state religion of the Roman empire. The institutionalizing of the Church required increased moral definition in order to "control" the "society." Authoritarian-ism, even totalitarianism, resulted as the hierarchical leaders, later speaking with the alleged infallibility of papal decree, determined the absolutism of moral formulations. Moral formulations are not absolute. God is absolute! What God is, only God is. We must not attribute an attribute of God to anything else. We must respect the non-transferrability of the divine attributes.

There are no distinct and definable moral absolutes apart from God in Jesus Christ, and deriving the expression of His absolute character.

Down through the centuries that followed, the Christian religion was characterized by ecclesiastical control over morality. As we noted in the beginning, that is how Christian religion, along with all religion, has come to be defined.

The Reformation of the sixteenth century simply re-formed the moralism, along with some theological formulations. The moralizing rigidity of John Calvin, the Swiss reformer, is an example of the failure of the reformers to grasp the dynamic restoration of God's grace in the living Lord Jesus.

So what has happened down through the centuries as the institutional church related to the world? How did Christian religion attempt to foist its social moralism upon society around it? Jacques Ellul notes how the church engaged in the

"perversion of making the gospel into law in order to respond to the challenge of successive outbursts of immorality and ethical disorder. Naturally Christians and the church could not fail to react to violence and sexuality and corruption. The mistake was to deal with these on the moral and legal plane instead of following the example of Paul, who always works through the moral question to

133

the spiritual question, gets back to the essence of the revelation in Christ, and from this derives some models of conduct that are consistent with faith and love. The church did not do this. It set itself on the same level as the world and treated moral matters on the moral plane. When a political question is treated merely as a political question, and a social question merely as a social question...the gospel becomes morality with a whitewash of theological terms."[21]

Contemporary issues where this same process continues to happen might include civil rights, abortion, euthanasia, etc.

The present situation in Christian ecclesiasticism is but a perpetuation of the ignorance and defiant independence that fails to differentiate between Christian behavior and morality. There is an almost wholesale failure to recognize the radical newness of new covenant Christianity and the dynamic of the life of Jesus Christ. Instead, religion reverts back to old covenant legalism and moralism. Repeatedly religion wants to construct a so-called "Christian Ethic" on the regulatory concept of the Ten Commandments. What an absurdity! What an abominable misrepresentation of Christianity! What an idolatrous substitution of law and moral code for grace, of formula and technique for freedom, of principles of goodness for God.

Christianity – Christian living – is the life of Jesus Christ lived out through us. Such is antithetical to all morality. To the extent that we accept, advocate or observe morality, and try to live and "be good" based on precepts or principles, rules or regulations, Christian living is excluded, the Christ-life is not being expressed, as they are mutually incompatible and exclusive. This is the point Paul makes to the Galatians: "I died to the Law (to morality), that I might live to God" (Gal. 2:19). "I do not nullify the grace of God; for if righteousness (goodness) comes through the Law (through morality), then Christ died needlessly" (Gal. 2:21). If you revert back to moral supplements, "Christ will be of no benefit to you," ...you have been severed from Christ..., you have fallen from grace" (Gal. 5:2-4), "the stumbling-block of the cross has been abolished" (Gal. 5:11). This is no slight matter! The issue at hand is the essence of the gospel!

Christianity is not morality! Christianity IS Christ!

Chapter Four

CHRISTIANITY IS *NOT* A BELIEF-SYSTEM

Remember the story that was related about Gautama Buddha in chaper one? Allow me to retell it again to set the stage for the point that needs to be made in this chapter.

Gautama Buddha lived some four hundred years prior to the birth of Jesus Christ. He was dying. Some of his devotees came to Buddha and asked how they should perpetuate his memory. "How should we share with the world the remembrance of you? How shall we memorialize you?" Buddha responded, "Don't bother! It is not me that matters, it is my teaching that should be propagated and adhered to throughout the world."

Does that seem self-effacing – a noble ideal to avoid ego-centricity? "Don't focus on me, just remember my teaching."

137

If Jesus Christ had said something like that, it would certainly legitimize what we see all around us in so-called "Christian religion" today. "Christian religion" has become the propagation of various understandings of Jesus' teaching as determined by various interpretations of the Bible. From what we observe in "Christian religion" today, it would appear that most who call themselves "Christians" must think that Jesus advocated the same thing that Buddha is alleged to have uttered.

Jesus Christ did not say anything like that! In fact, what Buddha said is contrary to everything Jesus taught, and everything recorded in the New Testament Scriptures. Jesus did not say, "Just remember My teaching." Jesus said, "I AM the way, the truth and the life." (John 14:6) "I AM the resurrection and the life." (John 11:25). Jesus Himself, the very Person and Life of Jesus Christ, is the essence of everything He came to bring to this world.

Christianity is not just another religion propagating an ideology. Christianity is not just another religion remembering the teaching of its founder. Christianity is not just another religion reiterating the propositional tenets of its founder's teaching, and calling such "truth." Christianity is not just another religion demanding conformity to a particular "belief-system" or data-base of doctrine.

The essence of Christianity is Jesus Christ. All of Christianity is inherent in Jesus, His Person and His continuing activity. Christianity functions only by the dynamic of the risen and living Lord Jesus. Christianity is the function of the Spirit of Christ as He continues to live in Christians.

It is a sad state of affairs in what is passed off as "Christian religion" today. There is almost total failure to discern that the essence of Christianity is Jesus Christ Himself. The essence of Christianity is not a standardized belief-system. The essence of Christianity is not a consensus of doctrine. The essence of Christianity is not commonality of creeds. Jesus Christ is the essence of Christianity.

Where did "Christian religion" go off track into thinking that consenting to, confessing and conforming to doctrinal data was what Christianity was all about? When did this "Christian religion" develop the idea that Christianity is the acceptance of a correct and orthodox belief-system?

Christians today seem to be abysmally ignorant of church history. A quick review of church history will assist in answering the questions just asked:

Jesus did not come to bring new information about God, about salvation, about love, about eternal life. Christ came to be Life to all mankind. He came as God, as salvation, as love. He came to restore mankind to what God intended in creation, and that by functioning as God in man, the spiritual dynamic of life.

The redemptive mission to make His life available took place, historically, in a world that was dominated by Jewish and Greek thinking. The Jews wanted to put everything into the context of an organized religion with rules and regulations. The Greeks were influenced by Plato and Aristotle with their abstract philosophical mind-set of metaphysics and logical patterns of thought.

So despite the clarity of Jesus' teaching, and the clear and simple record of the gospel dynamic of the life of Jesus Christ in the writings of Scripture by Paul, Peter, John, etc., these soon began to be interpreted in the contexts of religion and logical compartmentalization of human thought. The so-called "church fathers" of the first few centuries of Christianity had already reduced Christianity into moralistic and ethical religious rules and into creedalistic concepts of correct content of thought. They so quickly let go of the dynamic life of Jesus Christ as the essence of Christianity, and allowed it to become merely a belief-system.

The Roman Emperor, Constantine, solidified this static concept of Christianity even more in the early part of the fourth century. Constantine wanted to unify everything – government, economics, religion, "Christian thought", etc. He organized the Nicene Council in 325 A.D., bringing together these philosophically-based thinkers, theologians, to develop a rigid expression of "Christian belief." They compressed "Christian thought" into logical propositions of truth and orthodoxy and called it the "Nicene Creed," to which everyone who was called "Christian" was to give mental assent, or be regarded as a heretic.

By 325 A.D. Christianity had been perverted into a formulated and fixated belief system, demanding devotion to its doctrine. This process was progressively developed in the institutionalized Roman or Latin Church. T.F. Torrance refers to this epistemologically based rationalism as "the Latin heresy."[1]

Augustine lived and wrote in the century following the Nicene Council. His Augustinian theology, on which Calvin later based much of his theology, was extremely rationalistic, full of logical determinism with such ideas as strict divine predestination. Karl Barth referred to Augustinian theology as "sweet poison;"[2] "sweet" because it emphasized the sovereignty of God; "poison" because it was a system of logical and theological determinism.

The Roman empire disintegrated in about 500 A.D. The seven hundred year period from 200 B.C. to 500 A.D. is known as the "Classical Period" of Greek and Roman thought patterns. The following five hundred years, 500 A.D. to 1000 A.D. are known as the Dark Ages or Middle Ages. All thinking was related back statically to the Classical Period. No new thinking was encouraged or allowed – Dark Ages indeed!

Thomas Aquinas appeared as the Renaissance Period was picking up steam, but his Thomistic theology just placed "Christian thought" in a tight scholastic stronghold of the Roman Church. The Church was regarded as the mediator of God's thought. "Believe as the Pope and the Church advocates, or face the consequences!" Many did!

During the Renaissance Period the thinking of
"Christian religion" just followed along like a lap-dog to
the philosophers and scientists of that day (as it has
throughout most of its history.) Rene Descartes introduced
Cartesian doubt, "I think, therefore I am." Rationalistic
belief was the foremost criteria for being. Sir Isaac Newton
developed ideas of deterministic causalism, and these were
adapted into theology also.

In the sixteenth century the Reformation exploded with
Martin Luther, John Calvin, Ulrich Zwingli, and others. It
is called the "Reformation" because it re-formed the
religious structures that existed in "Christian religion" at
that time. But the birth of Protestantism did not restore the
centrality of the spiritual dynamic of Jesus Christ.
"Christian religion" was still regarded as essentially a
"belief-system," but instead of a singular formulated and
fixated belief-system in the Roman Church, it became
multiple factious and fractious belief-systems competing
with one another and beating on one another (both verbally
and physically.) Disagreeing on every minute point of
theology conceivable, they began to divide and sub-divide
into denominationalized belief-system organizations, each
believing that they had formulated and fixated their belief-

system in accord with God's thinking. There were Lutherans, Calvinists, Anabaptists and many others, all claiming to have the orthodox belief-system; all claiming to have figured-out what God, the "Great Theologue," believes and supposedly demands that all His adherents likewise believe.

Obviously there was not any recovery of the dynamic understanding of Christianity in the Protestant Reformation. Gene Edwards concludes, "The Reformation was neither revival nor restoration. The Reformation was an intellectual brawl."[3]

In the next century, in 1611 A.D., King James of England authorized what became known as *the Authorized Version*, better known as the *King James Version*, of an English translation of the Bible. The "Christian religion" of that day was still engaged in competing belief-systems.

King James hired translators to translate the Bible into English. The word for "teaching" in the English language of King James' time was "doctrine." The King James Version refers to the word "doctrine" 56 different times. But languages evolve, and the meanings of words change. So it is with the word "doctrine." Looking at a contemporary English dictionary you will discover that although "doctrine" used to mean "teaching" or "instruction," that definition is now regarded as "archaic" or "obsolete." What does the word "doctrine" mean in contemporary English? Webster's Collegiate Dictionary reads: "Doctrine – a principle accepted by a body of believers or adherents to a philosophy or school; principles of knowledge or a system of belief." "Doctrinaire – dictatorial or dogmatic." "Indoctrinate – to imbue with a partisan or sectarian opinion, point of view or principle." Synonyms used for "indoctrinate" include "propagandize, program, brainwash, infect, instill, inculcate, etc." Is it any wonder that newer English translations tend to avoid the word "doctrine"? The New American Standard Bible, for example, uses the word "doctrine" only fourteen times, and even those are probably a carry-over of the traditionalism of ecclesiastical terminology. The Greek words, *didache* and *didaskalia*, should be consistently translated "teaching," except when reference is being made to "man-made doctrines" (Eph. 4:14; Col. 2:22; etc.)

In contemporary English language "doctrine" has come to mean "a traditional belief-system as interpreted and accepted by a particular group of people." "Doctrinaire" means "to dogmatically assert a traditional belief-system as

145

interpreted and accepted by a particular group of people."
"Indoctrinate" implies "to propagandize or brainwash
others with this traditional belief-system as interpreted and
accepted by a particular group of people."

Such a definition was most certainly not what the
hearers intended when they listened to Jesus and "were
astonished at His doctrine" (Luke 4:32 - KJV). They were
not "astonished at His traditional belief-system," rather they
were "amazed at His teaching" (NASB). The teaching of
Jesus was the extending, the offering, the demonstration of
Himself – His Life. His teaching was Life-teaching. The
etymological root for the Greek word "teaching" had to do
with "extending the hand" or "offering oneself." To
demonstrate what is being taught; that is the way to teach
Life!

The fundamentalism and evangelicalism that
predominate in popular "Christian religion" in America
today tend to key in on "doctrine" as belief-system. That
may be the reason they often prefer to retain the King
James Version, and interpret the use of the word "doctrine"
throughout the New Testament as their particular brand of
formulated and fixated belief-system. These religious
doctrinarians continue to indoctrinate others and perpetuate

the factious and fractious denominationalism of differing belief-systems. Americans, with their fierce individualism and concepts of personal freedom, have elevated denominationalism to an all-time high, a real "religious science", with thousands of religious denominations, divided by disputed doctrinal belief-systems. Those involved in "Christian religion" today still think that Christianity is essentially consent to a particular doctrinal belief-system.

This is, in fact, the definition of "fundamentalism," a grouping of people who has rigidly determined the "fundamentals" of their acceptable doctrinal belief-system. "Fundamentalism" is a word much used today. The newspapers and news reports are full of references to "Muslim fundamentalists" in Iran, Libya, Lebanon, Egypt, etc.; "Hindu fundamentalists" in Sri Lanka; "Christian fundamentalists" barging at and bombing abortion clinics in the United States. Have you ever noticed that fundamentalists always fight? Why is that? They feel they have an obligation to defend the particular way they have stacked all of their doctrinal blocks in their belief-system.

The fundamentalist – "Christian religion" in general – has allowed doctrine, their belief-system, to become the supreme issue. "Doctrine" becomes their basis of fellowship, acceptance, security, bonding, etc. It is a tragic misrepresentation of the Church when the basis of our commonality is calculated by doctrinal agreement, rather than the indwelling Lord Jesus Christ; when uniformity of doctrine is the primary issue instead of unity in Christ. How sad when much of what is called "Christian preaching" is but tirades against so-called "heretics" who do not stack the doctrinal fundamentals of their belief-system just like we do!

Doctrine has been deified in "Christian religion" today. Doctrine has become their "god." It is a gross form of idolatry when one's properly-aligned stack of doctrinal ideas is elevated and revered to the extent that it must be defended at all costs, even to the point of terrorism, even to the point of dying for it.

God alone is absolute and immutable. His attributes are exclusive to Himself. What God is, only God is. To attribute God's attributes to our doctrine and determine that our doctrine is absolute and unchangeable is to deify doctrine, and to engage in the absolutism that is indicative of fundamentalistic religion around the world.

The Scottish preacher and teacher, James S. Stewart, wrote these words: "Those who have succeeded in defining doctrine most closely, have lost Christ most completely."[4]

Doctrines, belief-systems, will always be the focus of religion, but not of Christianity. Christianity is Christ! Jesus' teaching was about Himself. He is the essence of Christian teaching, contrary to what Buddha said about his religion.

In Christianity, TRUTH is a Person, Jesus Christ. "Truth" is not just propositional truth statements within a belief-system of doctrinal theology by which orthodoxy is rationalistically determined. Jesus Christ is Truth! Jesus Christ is our Life! He is so exclusively; there is no other Way! John 14:6 - "I AM the way, the truth and the life."

Christianity is not a belief-system. Christianity is Christ!

Chapter Five

CHRISTIANITY IS *NOT* EPISTEMOLOGY

Have you heard of "the epistemological heresy"? Though the phrase may be novel, the heresy is nothing new. It is just a new title on an old problem. In fact, the "epistemological heresy" may be the underlying heresy of all heresies, "the mother of all heresies." This particular heresy is so subtle and pervasive that most who would call themselves "Christians" have inadvertently adapted to its heretical presuppositions and are unable to recognize the extent to which they have adopted its premises. Most of Western Christian theology has been infected by the mind-set of this heresy.

Throughout the centuries of Christian thought there have been Christian thinkers who have honestly and spiritually maintained the distinctiveness of the Christian message. Those outside of the Christian faith have often reacted to the Christian presentation and proclamation, finding particularly offensive the legitimate assertions of exclusivity concerning the singular reconciliation of man with God through Jesus Christ. As the Christian presentation is typically argued, though, the offense to non-Christian inquirers may be quite valid. If the argument is simply that my belief-system is superior to your belief-system (and any other belief-system), then such an offensive (double entendre intended) approach to exclusivism is indeed pompous and elitist.

When Christians proudly assert sole claim to absolute information and exact understanding of precise precepts of moral standards, they have set themselves up as gods on their own playground. When Christian presentation stoops to the level of mere apologetic reasoning and argument concerning tenets of mental assent, then the relativistic battleground is but a gory picture of the blind beating out the brains of the blind.

Perhaps the foregoing has given the reader a glimpse of what the "evangelical heresy" might entail. Further explanation will first require closer definition.

Defining Terms

"Epistemology" is a philosophical term etymologically derived from three Greek words: (1) *epi* meaning "upon" or "on"; (2) *histemi* meaning "to stand"; (3) *logos* meaning "word," and indicating "logical consideration of or study of." The Greek word *epistamai* referred to the process of acquiring knowledge and understanding, as well as the significance of such information. Epistemology refers to the considerations of what we stand upon for our understanding. How do we know what we know? Why do we believe what we believe? Where do we take our stand concerning the opinions that we claim to believe and to know? These are the considerations of epistemology.

The New Testament contains several usages of the Greek word *epistamai*. A couple of examples should suffice to document such.

In the "faith chapter" of Hebrews 11, the writer explains that "by faith Abraham, when he was called, obeyed by going out..., not knowing (*epistamenos*) where he was going" (Heb. 11:8). Abraham did not have the logistics, the chronology, the itinerary of his journey all logically established. The details of his sojourn were not epistemologically determined in human logic categories, but instead he trusted God in faith.

Writing to Timothy, Paul indicates that "if anyone does not agree with...the teaching conforming to godliness, he is conceited (puffed up) and understands (*epistamenos*) nothing" (I Tim. 6:3,4). Paul's argument seems to be that the teaching of the Christian life is based on the faith-derivative of God's character expressed in human behavior. To fail to understand and agree with this is to "stand upon" insubstantial understanding. Although such a person may have their epistemological belief-system all systematized and categorized, theologized and dogmatized, he takes his "stand upon" something other than the dynamic person of Jesus Christ.

Additional Greek words are used in the New Testament to refer to "knowledge" and "understanding," including the words *eideo* and *gnosis*. To the Corinthians Paul notes that "knowledge (*gnosis*) makes arrogant (puffs up), but love edifies" (I Cor. 8:1). Later in the same epistle he writes, "if I know (*eido*) all mysteries and all knowledge (*gnosin*)...but do not have love, I am nothing" (I Cor. 13:2). Metaphysical understanding and intellectual understanding acquired epistemologically are not God's ultimate objective for man. Rather, God wants His character of love to be expressed behaviorally. Paul explains that his prayer for the Ephesians is that they might "know (*gnonai*) the love of God which surpasses knowledge (*gnoseos*)" (Eph. 3:19).

Jesus indicted the Jewish Pharisees by charging, "You search the Scriptures, because you think that in them you have eternal life; and it is these that bear witness of Me; and you are unwilling to come to Me, that you may have life" (John 5:39,40). The written statements of factual information about history and theology contained in the Biblical record and upon which religious people take their stand to develop a belief-system and a doctrinal position, constitute only a foundational basis of epistemological understanding. Jesus considered such totally insufficient as the basis for the divine reality that He was making available in Himself. He was making His own divine being, His own life, available for the restoration of functional mankind.

Epistemological understanding is inadequate to comprehend the divine reality that is the essence of Christianity. The objective of the Christian message is not to encourage people to receive and accumulate and assent to information, but rather to receive the very Being of God into themselves (John 1:12) and allow Jesus Christ to be their life (Col. 3:4).

The essence of Christianity is to be identified as ontological rather than epistemological. "Ontology" is etymologically derived from two Greek words: (1) *ontos* meaning "being." (2) *logos* meaning "word," and indicating "logical consideration of or study of." "Ontology" refers to the philosophical study of being. In its broadest usage "ontology" considers the entire issue of being and existence in general. More specifically, we are employing "ontology" as referring to the divine Being of the Creator God, and His personal relation to His created beings; the relation of the God-Being and human beings. The personal Being of God, the I AM (Exod. 3:14), and His relationship with human beings must be considered ontologically rather than merely epistemologically. The knowledge being considered is not just the knowledge of impersonal factual data and information, but the personal knowing of personal beings in personal relationship.

The purpose of this study, then, is to emphasize the ontological considerations that must be foremost in Christian reasoning. This is never to deny though that there is an epistemologically based understanding that is foundational to Christianity. There are historically dated events and theological interpretations of those events that form the foundation for Christian understanding. They are documentable and logical. Christianity is not just a subjective, mystical experiencing of supernatural, metaphysical being with existential significance. Such is the false accusation of secular epistemological extremists. The opposing extreme is to camp with the religious epistemologists who view Christianity as but an historical society for the remembrance of Jesus' birth, life, death and resurrection, or as but a theological society for the interpretation of those events. To present Christianity with an exclusively epistemological emphasis is equally extremist as presenting it as exclusively existential experientialism. Avoiding the extremes, we want to understand the ontological reality of Christianity, how the very Being of God, His life, His character is present in the Christian by the indwelling spiritual presence of the Spirit of Christ, and how He desires to live out His life and express His character in our behavior.

An Historical Survey

The Creator-God created the creature-man in such a way as to encourage the free-flow of the active expression of God's character in the behavior of man. The freedom for such function is symbolized by the option of the freely chosen "tree of life" (Gen. 2:9,16). In such a receptive faith-choice man would allow for the grace expression of God's activity, thus imaging God's character in visible behavior. This ontological flow of divine Being expressed within and through humanity was the Creator's intent, so as to glorify Himself within His creation (Isa. 43:7; 48:11).

The fall of man into sin indicates the choice that mankind made collectively "in Adam." It was a choice to disallow the ontic flow of divinity expressed in humanity, to sever that unique relationship of Divine Being expressed in the human being. Man was divorced from the spiritual unity of relationship he had with God, sacrificing his spiritual identity, nature, image, etc., which were contingent on that relationship. Instead man chose the lie of independent determination of right, good, truth, etc., with the fallacious epistemological understanding that he could determine from his own self-centered perspective what is true, good and right.

The history of mankind is replete with a confusion of opinions as men have advocated competing ideologies to attempt to explain themselves and their universe. Their quest for identity and meaning, for certainty and security, are but an ongoing enactment of Babel with semantic and interpretive diversities *ad infinitum.*

Greek philosophers in particular were adept at articulating reasoned explanations of universal principles. Socratic dialecticism, Platonic dualism, Aristotelian rationalism all indicate the epistemological base of the Greek philosophers which has had such a lasting effect on Western thought and religion.

"In the fullness of time" (Gal. 4:4), Jesus Christ, the God-man, was vested into the historical situation of mankind by the incarnation. As the "I AM" (Exod. 3:14) Being of God, He repeatedly verbalized such in the *ego eimi* declarations recorded particularly in John's gospel (John 6:35; 8:12,58; 10:9,11; 11:25; 14:6; 15:1). He came as man to take the sin of man, to vicariously bear the death consequences of sin as man, in order to restore mankind with His divine life, the restoration of functional humanity by the ontological presence of the Spirit of Christ within the spirit of man. This is the grace distinctive of

159

Christianity wherein the radical uniqueness of the divine action (salvation, justification, sanctification, etc.) is necessarily derived out of, and is vital expression of, the divine Being in Christ. The ontological connection and association of God and man is restored in Christ.

The explanation of this living presence of God in man by the risen Lord Jesus was not a simple matter since the original proclamation was set in the context of Jewish religion. Epistemological mind-set was rigidly fixed in their law-based doctrinalism and moralism.

The Greek wisdom of Gnosticism was also a formidable antagonist to nascent Christian presentation. A dualism of spirit and matter alongside of a dualism of cause and effect via spiritual emanations created a pseudo-balance of epistemological and experiential understanding.

Whereas the first century polarization was primarily a breaking free from identification with Jewish religion, the concerns of the Christian thinkers in the second, third and fourth centuries was primarily in reaction to Greek Gnosticism. Reactions often produce opposite extremes as the pendulum swings the other way, and so it was that the ontic distinctive of Christianity was overshadowed by the epistemological concerns of doctrine and morality, as

160

evidenced in the writings of the church fathers and their reversion to legalism. The ensuing creedalizing of a Christian belief-system has been referred to as "the Latin heresy,"[1] but we are herewith using the broader designation of "the epistemological heresy."

As the institutional church proceeded into the Medieval period the preservation of doctrinal orthodoxy was regarded as paramount. Inquisitions were conducted to combat error and heretical opinions, with every means employed to ostracize, excommunicate and murder those who disagreed.

The Protestant Reformation was but a re-forming of theological and ethical reasoning. John Calvin's theological systematizing in his *Institutes of the Christian Religion* relied heavily on Augustinian determinism and the closed-system of epistemic thought Augustine employed. Calvin's ethics were likewise devoid of ontic understanding.

The history of Protestantism is but a melee of doctrinal argumentation as the denominationalized systematic theologians contend for their interpretations. The so-called Enlightenment only exacerbated the epistemic warfare with its emphasis on rationalism and the determination of truth by deductive logic and propositional conclusions.

161

Has anything changed? Christian religion today is mired in doctrinal dispute. They argue over the length of one's *ordo salutis* in the "Lordship salvation" debate. They banter about the legitimacy of charismatic experientialism. They attempt to defend their historical and theological assertions with apologetic proofs. Contemporary fundamentalism and evangelicalism are so entrenched in the "epistemological heresy" that their ideologies have become idolatry, and they proceed to worship the Baal of natural thinking rather than God in Christ.

Making the Distinction

It is imperative that we make the distinction between an epistemological base of knowing and perceiving action and an ontological base of knowing and perceiving action. Christianity is not essentially assent to or belief in tenets of truth, but rather receptivity to and participation in the activity of the Being of the One who is Truth (John 14:6). Jesus did not say, "I came that you might have orthodox beliefs and defend them apologetically." He said, "I came that you might have life (the very Being of God) and have such more abundantly (in the abundant expression of God's character in our behavior). (John 10:10)

The religion of "natural man" inevitably slides toward epistemological knowledge, towards knowledge of external data formulated in propositional truth statements. These "articles of faith" are defended most adamantly as essential doctrines of Christian catechism.

When the reason of man is thus deified, it spawns innumerable ideas, concepts, opinions, thoughts, doctrines, prejudices, etc. These mental constructs (such as the "idea of God" or the "idea of salvation") tend to become self-existent entities, autonomous tenets, which develop a history of their own, with a separate self-generative function. Thus they are evaluated, plotted, charted, analyzed, modified, altered and criticized.

Natural theology develops an "idea about God" by logical deduction. "He must be, therefore He is." It is an attempt to know God apart from God. Such reasoning may even arrive at a concept of a monotheistic God who is infinitely personal and loving, with an only-begotten Son who was willing to be incarnated and to give His life in crucifixion. Such an "idea of God" and "idea of salvation" can still be detached from any personal knowing of the Living God. If so it remains an idolatrous false-image carved in the mind of man. Natural theology is anathema!

163

God can be known only in the personal self-revelation of Himself. More specifically, God's revelation is made by the Son (Luke 10:22). God is known personally and relationally in an ontological bond, a spiritual union (I Cor. 6:17). God does not reveal some "thing" about Himself in order to make available some "thing" (such as holiness, goodness, love, peace, etc.); rather He reveals Himself, His Being, for that which He desires to give is Himself, His Being in action in man.

Our theology must always commence with who God is, not with His decrees, His will or His laws. God does what He does because He is who He is, not because He has decreed a plan, developed a principle, determined a precept, and set these in motion in deistic detachment.

The Being of God and the act of God must remain connected. They must always cohere. There is no act of God apart from His Being. His Being is always dynamically involved in His act. His doing is always the dynamic expression of His Being. The activity of God is derived out of His Being, *ek theos*. "God is love" (I John 4:8,16); the active expression of love is *ek theos* (I John 4:7), only and always.

164

God is the very content of all that He does. The divine action (whether salvation, justification, sanctification, etc.) is necessarily derived out of, and is the vital expression of, the divine Being in Christ. Those who would know God's benefits and God's blessings must recognize that God's benefits to man cannot be known apart from His functional Being. God's blessing is to bless us with Himself. God "has blessed us with every spiritual blessing in heavenly places in Christ" (Eph 1:3), who is the "summing up of all things" (Eph. 1:10).

Who God is and what God does are inseparable. His Being and His act must ever remain united. This is the point that epistemology fails to understand. Inherent in the rationalistic approach is a "separated concept" that detaches the divine Actuator from the divine activity. When natural theology deals merely with "ideas" and "concepts," then the "idea of God" cannot be equated or conjoined with the "idea" of divine effects (ex. salvation, sanctification, etc.). They stand alone, autonomously self-existent with independent functions. There is an isolation of divine effect that is explainable only as the mechanical result of the "idea of God." Separated into such constituent parts, Christian activity is construed as conferment or endowment

165

of benefits. The divine act is disconnected from the divine Actor. Christian realities are viewed as products, commodities, "goods," or "services." A professor writes in a purportedly academic theological journal: "God has made payment for 'services' provided through Jesus Christ."[2] "...an individual comes to Jesus...so he can receive what Jesus offers."[3] "...salvation, security, assurance...He (Jesus) must deliver them."[4]

Misconceptions of this kind are based on an epistemological dualism of a dissected cause and effect. In the closed mechanistic system of Newtonian science, for example, there is a linear thought process that views empirical effects as inevitable results of necessary cosmic laws. The effect can be traced back to the cause but never to be considered one with the cause. The same epistemological dualism is seen in religious and theological reasoning. Religious effects may be traced to necessary universal spiritual "laws" such as the "law of faith" or the "law of prayer." Often there are legal and judicial concepts of Christ's benefits, as in the popular theological explanation of justification. Cause and effect are split one from the other. There may be mechanical source leading to static logical effect, or mythological source leading to ecstatic psychological effect, but there remains a "separated concept," both epistemologically or experientially.

The radical uniqueness of Christianity is in the ontological connection and cohesion of the divine cause or source and the divine effect. God, the divine source effects the expression of His Being. The divine effect is only as God sources such by His grace. God can and must be identified with, even equated with, His effects. His effects are the activity of His Being.

Christian theology must maintain the oneness of spiritual activity with the Spirit-source – God within His acts. There is no spiritual reality to that effected apart from the dynamic source-reality of Divine Being. To separate benefit from Being is to construct a false religious image which is not the vital living activity of God in Christ. Any religious act or idea, viewed apart from what God is doing because He is who He is, operating by His grace, expressing Himself by His Son, Jesus Christ, is necessarily sterile, static and severed from reality, as well as idolatrous, abominable and anathema.

Derivative man never generates Christian activity, or any activity for that matter, for the corresponding theodicy must understand the ontic connection and association of the

167

unregenerate person identified with the Evil one and manifesting his character of evil. The Christian, identified with God in Christ, is free to be functional human being in ontic relationship with the divine Being. In that contingency of faith-receptivity, God comes to dwell personally in man thereby giving to man being, nature, identity and image in interpersonal relationship with Himself, with His Son, and activating through man the expression of His own character unto His own glory.

Christianity demands an ontological understanding with an indivisible coinherence of God's Being and His act. The dynamism of Christian grace wherein the activity of the risen Lord Jesus is operative by the Spirit is the heartbeat of Christianity. The very person and life of the resurrected Christ dwells in the Christian (II Cor. 13:5; Gal. 2:20; Col. 1:27), and that in order to manifest His life in our mortal bodies (II Cor. 4:10,11). Thus the dynamic function of God is restored within humanity, as He manifests His Being in the human being.

Examples

It will be instructive to consider a few basic themes of Christian teaching to consider the necessity of maintaining the connectedness of God and His working in Christ, and at the same time to expose examples of the disjuncture of such in popular evangelical teaching, resulting in deistic detachment and Trinitarian deficiency.

"Gospel"

Zane Hodges refers to "the gospel under siege"[5] and John MacArthur decries the "erosion of the gospel,"[6] but in their antagonism they both conceive of the gospel as a corpus of doctrinal truths. Joining the fray, Darrell Bock asserts that the "gospel is a precious truth"[7] which must be "handled properly."[8] Dave Hunt concludes that "the gospel...has three basic elements: (1) Who Christ is. (2) Who we are. (3) What Christ's death accomplished."[9] This three-point information-package is then said to "save those who believe it. Nothing else will save."[10] He goes on to speak disparagingly of those who merely "receive Jesus."[11] From his rationalistic perch, John W. Robbins explains that "the gospel is a creed. If we do not believe the creed, we do not believe Christ."[12] Robbins continues by saying, "Christ identified Himself with His words. The words and the Word are identical."[13] If Jesus' words, His teaching, His propositional and sentential instruction, are the formulation of the gospel, then it would be legitimate to refer to "the gospel according to Jesus," as does John MacArthur.[14] In so doing, though, the gospel is separated from Jesus Christ and the "separated concept" of epistemology is evident. The gospel is thus detached from the active Being of God and devalued to but one belief-system among many, albeit the divinely revealed teaching rather than human wisdom.

The "good news" of the gospel is Jesus Christ! The gospel is not logical propositions, but the living Person of God in Christ. It is "good news" indeed that God has made available in His Son the restoration of the vital dynamic of His divine Being, that by the indwelling presence and activity of the risen and living Lord Jesus. Only in such an ontological connection is the divine intent of the gospel preserved. Gerhardt Friedrich explains that "the gospel and its content are one;"[15] "the risen Lord is the *auctor evangelii*,"[16] the origination and enactment of the gospel.

"Salvation"

The gospel is the dynamic power of God unto salvation (Rom. 1:16). Since the gospel is Jesus, and Christ is the power of God (I Cor. 1:24), the saving activity of God must not be disassociated from the function of the Savior.

Contemporary evangelical thought refers time and again to Jesus "bringing" and "delivering"[17] salvation, as if salvation were the beneficial product which Jesus the "delivery-boy" came to provide. Darrell Bock refers to Jesus as "the divine dispenser of salvation,"[18] apparently casting Jesus into a role similar to a bubble-gum dispenser or a medical dispensary. How often have you heard someone refer to another who allegedly "got saved," as if salvation were some "thing" that we get and possess or some static experience or event? These epistemological concepts rend salvation from the necessary coherence with the Savior, so that the historical redemptive work of the Savior is detached and separated from the present experience of salvation. The risen and living Lord Jesus and His on-going "saving life" (Rom. 5:10) become but an unnecessary redundancy, for salvation stands alone as a mechanical divine effect of an historically enacted event. God forbid that such should be promulgated in the name of Christianity!

Salvation cannot be separated from the Savior. There is no salvation apart from the ongoing, continuous, dynamic saving life and action of Jesus the Savior. The divine source and the salvific effect are combined. His saving activity is Himself in action. Only when the Savior, Jesus Christ, is functionally operative in the Christian do we participate in the salvation process, being made safe from dysfunctional and misused humanity in order to function as God intended by His Being functioning in mankind. Salvation must be conjoined ontologically with the living Savior.

"Grace"

If we accept the popular definition of "grace" as a "gift" or an "undeserved favor," the factor of epistemological separation is again obvious. The divine Giver is set apart from the gift. An ontological consideration of grace recognizes that all that God gives is Himself, His own Being in action.

Grace is sometimes perceived as a mechanical instrument of causality, the "force" God employs to accomplish His desires. Grace has been viewed as the "threshold factor" that effected redemption which then allows for the individual effect of conversion. Some have explained grace as some "thing" God imparts as the parcels of His sufficiency are needed. Theologians have referred to the "infusion of grace," "the means of grace," the ecclesiastical "dispensing of grace." All of these are attempts to quantify grace, disassociating grace from God.

Grace is indivisible from God Himself. Grace is the self-giving of God in His Son, Jesus Christ. "Grace is realized through Jesus Christ" (John 1:17), and there is no grace apart from Christ. God does not act *en dissecio* or *en partio*. He does not act apart from who He is, apart from Jesus Christ and the Holy Spirit.

This divine expression of the Oneness of His triune Being can be applied to all other Christian themes also. Righteousness (justification) cannot be disjoined from Jesus Christ, the Righteous One (I John 2:1). Godliness cannot be isolated from the dynamic expression of God's character. Sanctification cannot be separated from the Holy One, active by His Holy Spirit.

The gospel of salvation by God's grace is ontologically established in the Being of God expressed in His acts. The epistemological heresy that statically separates Christianity from Christ, and salvation from the Savior, must be repudiated.

Christians must cease to offer a "false bill of goods," an epistemological package of propositional truths and alleged spiritual benefits detached from the dynamic of God's grace and the living Lord Jesus. To explain the ontological reality of God's Being functioning in man relationally, Jesus Christ living in the Christian and working out salvation through the Christian, is most difficult since fallen man is accustomed to thinking only in natural epistemological categories. Even so, the Christian is compelled from within to share Jesus Christ, trusting that in the midst of such presentation God will ontologically reveal Himself to others by the Spirit of Christ.

Chapter Six

CHRISTIANITY IS *NOT* ROLE-PLAYING

The famous bard from Avon, William Shakespeare, wrote into the script of his play, *As You Like It*, these lines,

> "All the world's a stage,
> And all the men and women merely players.
> They have their exits and their entrances,
> And one man in his time plays many parts."[1]

Is it true that "all the world's a stage," and life is "playing various parts" or roles? The world-system seems to be built on the pretense of playing roles. All men and women are either actors or actresses. Some work back-stage, some have bit-parts, some have supporting roles, and all aspire to achieve a star-role.

There is a basic philosophy that pervades the thinking of our society today which regards everything as a "show," a "production," a "performance." It is all "staged" and

175

orchestrated and choreographed by the Producer/Director named "Fate." "The Show must go on!"

In this humanistic drama of human existence all the players develop a "false persona." It's a ruse. It's a fake. It's all fiction. W. Somerset Maughn, in his work, *The Summing Up*, writes, "The drama is make-believe. It does not deal with truth, but with effect."[2] What he seems to be saying is that the drama is not reality or truth. The projected symbol and its effect on the audience is all that matters.

Talk-show host, Rush Limbaugh, has pointed out that there is an abundance of unreality on the political stage in our society today. He has pointed out the hypocrisy of "symbol over substance," and playing for the effect that something has upon others. All that seems to matter is the existential perception of the individual.

The concept of life as "role-playing" has permeated so much of our society today. Take, for example, the societal issue of homosexuality. When two men enter into what they call a "relationship," they are role-playing. Usually one assumes the role of the husband, and the other assumes the role of the wife. Neither is a real man. A real man relates to a woman as God intended between husband and wife. The one who plays the role of the husband in the homosexual relationship is not a real male, and the one who plays the role of the wife in the homosexual relationship is not a real female (obviously). It is a perverse form of role-playing. Why is it that homosexuals are so often attracted to, and found within, the fine-arts community? Ex.: actors, actresses, musicians, artists, dancers. Is it because these often engage in the unreality of role-playing?

The social issue of feminism looms large in our society today. They are concerned about gender-roles. Thinking that "wife" and "mother" are just roles that women play, they aspire to the star-role of being C.E.O. of the company or President of the United States. Will that make them more of a woman? ...more female? ...more feminine? It will not. It will only set them up as another kind of actress, playing another role. Radical feminist theology wants to call God "Mother" or "It." They fallaciously think that "Father" is just a role that God plays, and they want to recast His role. Little do they realize that to say "God is our Father," is to explain and give meaning to Divine provision, protection, propagation of life, etc. It is not just a title role. Radical feminism mistakenly casts everything into the role-playing of gender roles.

The contemporary psychologism of identifying dysfunctional families and their inter-relational traits, likewise casts all family dynamics into role-playing. Family members are regarded as playing different roles, such as "codependent enabler," the "scapegoat child," etc. If the relationship of a family is considered only as different members playing different roles, it will be dysfunctional indeed.

A more recent phenomenon in the contemporary electronic and digital world is the "virtual reality" communities wherein role-playing is elevated to a comprehensive and all-encompassing "second life." Participants fashion their own digidentity (digital + identity), known as an "avatar," and engage in business, education, religion, and every other projection of human life. The interaction of digital relationships even includes elaborate marriage ceremonies to another role-playing "avatar." Many computer participants have become so enamored and addicted to the "virtual reality" universe that they have lost touch with the reality of the real world.

Is religion any different? Religion just presents mankind with another stage on which to engage in yet another avenue of "role-playing." Sometimes this is nothing more than assuming the role of audience or participant in the Sunday morning "production" of a worship "performance." Staged Christianity puts on the show! It is all symbol without substance. When it is over and the curtain closes, everyone takes off their costumes and their masks and their make-up, and goes home until the next production, feeling no need to maintain the role except when they are on the religious stage. John Calvin refers to such religious actors, noting that "in all ages there have been certain worshippers of God who have worshiped him like stage-players, whose holiness did wholly consist in gestures and vain pomps."₃

Sometimes religion casts itself as a lifestyle of role-playing. The convert assumes the identity of a "Christian" on the religious stage. They are expected to play the role and stay "in character." They repeat their lines, parrot their part, and play their role. They "go through the motions" knowing that the rituals are not reality. Religion is just a "bit-part" they play in life. It's not real. They are wearing masks and costumes. It is hypocrisy! Their continuation in such makes them enablers to one another in the fictional drama that they are all play-acting, and they become codependent to one another's sins in dysfunctional religion.

Activistic religion has encouraged its cast to play various roles in support of chosen causes. Often it is the "crusader role" against abortion, pornography or specified social evils. Other times it may be the "Good Samaritan role," serving in a soup-kitchen or at a rescue mission. The role is played with the utmost of sincerity as it is regarded as the reality of their religion.

In order to play the role in the religious drama, there must be a supporting cast to make the play work. Everyone has to play the game together, and be willing to act-out the same scenario, longing for the applause of a job well-done. Without such the individualized hypocrisy becomes a sham! The ecclesiastical community of the institutional church has served as the supporting cast for this religious role-playing.

Religion is a simulated reality – role-playing. The misnomer of "Christian religion" has long encouraged its cast to play the role of a Christian. People are encouraged to "act like a Christian." The effect upon others is emphasized to the neglect of reality.

Christianity, as differentiated from "Christian religion," is not role-playing! The Christian identifies in spiritual solidarity with Jesus Christ, who becomes his/her life, and the basis of their new identity as a "Christ-one," a Christian. "If anyone is in Christ, he is a new creature; old things have passed away, behold all thing have become new" (II Cor. 5:17). The Christian does not have an assumed identity, but the real identity wherein "Christ lives in me" (Gal. 2:20). The Christian is not playing a role, but the essential reality of the life of Jesus Christ indwells within and is to function through his/her behavior. The ontological Being of Jesus Christ, the "I AM," constitutes who we are and what we do. It is an actual living-out of the life of Jesus Christ in the Christian's behavior.

It is not "make-believe." Christianity is real-believe. Faith involves the receptivity of the activity of the life of Jesus Christ in the believer. It is the receptivity of divine reality; the Being of Christ expressed in our behavior.

There is a vast difference between acting out a role or part, and acting in our behavior by the expression of the life of Jesus Christ lived out through us. Trying to "stay in character" throughout the religious "performance" is very difficult and demanding, but Jesus Christ wants to "manifest His life in our mortal bodies" (II Cor. 4:10,11), His character in our behavior. We are not called to the false-persona of an actor or actress, but to the Reality of the Person of Jesus Christ lived out through man.

This reality of an ontological identity with Christ is relational, first in the personal relationship the Christian has with Jesus Christ, and secondly in the relational community of the Church wherein we need each other in order to encourage one another (Heb. 10:25) in the living out of our new identity. The Church is not merely a "supportive cast for our role-playing;" it is the extended Body that shares in the very Life of Jesus Christ that forms our identity as "Christ-ones." We are "in Him" together, sharing His Life, and encouraging one another to behave like who we have really and spiritually become. This genuine mutuality and unity allows for no masks of hypocrisy, but allows us to "drop our guard" in true transparency in order to live out His life together.

Christianity is not role-playing! Christianity is the reality of the Person of Jesus Christ lived out in Christian behavior.

Chapter Seven

CHRISTIANITY IS *NOT* AN ...ISM

In the first chapter we sought to explain that Christianity is not a religion, despite the fact that the misnomer of "Christian religion" does exist today. The failure to differentiate between Christianity and religion has created much confusion and obfuscation in the thinking of both Christians and non-Christians. It has become necessary to explain that the Christian religion, sometimes referred to as "Christendom," is the organized institutional entity that many also mistakenly refer to as the "Church." That is why Soren Kierkegaard wrote a book entitled *Attack on Christendom*, and explained that

> "Christendom is an effort of the human race to go back to walking on all fours, to get rid of Christianity, to do it knavishly under the pretext that this is Christianity, claiming that it is Christianity perfected.[1]

> The Christianity of Christendom...takes away from Christianity the offense, the paradox, etc., and instead of that introduces probability, the plainly comprehensible. That is, it transforms Christianity into something entirely different from what it is in the New Testament, yea, into exactly the opposite; and this is the Christianity of Christendom, of us men."[2]

Christian religion is the sociological movement that is comprised of formulated belief-systems and morality patterns, and is structured into hierarchical political organizations. Christianity, on the other hand, is the vital dynamic of the Spirit of Christ in those who are receptive to Him by faith. A Christian is a "Christ-one," identified in spiritual union with Jesus Christ, and Christianity is "Christ-in-you-ity" (cf. Col. 1:27; II Cor. 13:5), as the Spirit of Christ indwells the spirit of each Christian individual (Rom. 8:9).

Our explanations are further complicated when we recognize that the English word "Christianity" has as its equivalent in the French language, the word *"christianisme."* This would tend to imply that Christianity is some form of philosophical ...ism. Such is not the case. Christianity is not an ...ism! Jacques Ellul, a French writer, wrote a book entitled *La Subversion du Christianisme*. It was later translated into English as *The Subversion of Christianity*,[3] but this was misleading to some English

184

readers who did not realize the double entendre of the title, and thus thought that Ellul was engaged in Christian-bashing. God forbid, for Ellul was an extremely astute Christian who did, indeed, critically expose Christian religion, but admirably expounded the reality of Christianity in the living Lord Jesus Christ. In fact, it was Jacques Ellul who, in the aforementioned book, sought to explain that Christianity is not an ...ism, and thus provided the germinal idea for this chapter. It will be instructive to quote what he wrote, and allow it to serve as a springboard for our further elucidation.

"A word ending in 'ism' denotes an ideological or doctrinal trend deriving from a philosophy. Thus we have positivism, socialism, republicanism, spiritualism, idealism, materialism, etc. None of these words, however, denotes the philosophy itself. In fact, it might be directly opposed to it. Marx and Kierkegaard both tried to prevent their thinking from being reduced to an ideological mechanism. But they could not stop their successors from freezing their living thought into one (or many) systems, and in this way an ideology arose. Even Sartre accepts the term existentialism without seeing how it perverts what he is saying. The moment the mutation takes place from existential thinking to existentialism, a living stream is transformed into a more or less regulated and stagnant irrigation channel, and as the thought moves further and further away from the source it becomes banal and familiar.

The suffix 'ism' injects something new into a well-marked and well-defined complex. As originality is eliminated and replaced by commonplaces, the life and thought lose their radical and coherent character. The well-defined complex is now vague and fluid. Passages are dug out in all directions. From the point of departure various possibilities open up for exploitation, and they are in fact utilized. There thus comes into being a curious complex formed of many tendencies, often contradictory but all covered by the relevant 'ism.' In a final loosening of the original knot of life and thought, which are generally united in the creator and his immediate disciples, the 'ism' sometimes takes the form of a practical sociological trend, a type of organization or mass movement, such as socialism, communism, royalism, or republicanism.

At this point there is an even greater distance between the rock of the first life and thought and the sandy wastes that now engulf it. Marxism and what has been derived from it for a whole century have nothing in common. It is the same whenever an 'ism' is made in the name of some creator, such as Thomism, Lutheranism, or Rousseauism. It seems that in each case the deviation and subversion mentioned are typical of the Western world. We need not go into that here. The only point is that the 'ism' aspect of Christianity is not peculiar to it. Similar results occur in many other cases. Nevertheless, the perversion or subversion here is much more vast and aberrant and incomprehensible than any of the others."[4]

Ellul is correct in asserting that the attempted reduction of Christianity into an ...ism is a greater perversion than any other. The living reality of the divine life of Jesus Christ that constitutes Christianity, cannot be killed and compressed into a closed casket of an ideological construct. The theories and concepts of man can, and are, boiled down into ...isms, but how can the ontological dynamic of the infinite Living God be compressed into a humanly manageable package of thought? Impossible, except it be decimated and destroyed, having been reduced to something that no longer represents the reality of the expression of God in Jesus Christ.

The Formulating of ...isms

It is the natural propensity of man to attempt to get everything figured out with finite reasoning. This is particularly true of man in Western civilization, following in the footsteps of Aristotelian reasoning, and seeking to explain all phenomena in the linear logic of direct cause and effect. Man wants to turn his observations into syllogisms and rational laws based on deductive inferences and inductive persuasion.

The philosophers and the theologians, in particular, have served as thought-mechanics to ratchet and wrench human thought into ideological constructs. They are not content to allow the conceptual artists of poetry and drama and music to express ideas in abstraction. The logicians can allow for no paradoxes or antinomies that are against the law of reason. Their minds short-circuit whenever there are loose-ends of thought that cannot be tied-down into an outline of reasonable categories. Contrary to Eastern thinkers who are more prone to accept a both-and explanation rather than a polarized either-or explanation, the Western thinkers have a difficult time accepting the balance of a dialectic tension. Western philosophy and theology has thus tended to analyze, categorize, compartmentalize and systematize their thought into tightly formulated structures, propagated in academic disciplines such as systematic or dogmatic theology. They have a lust for understanding and certainty that cannot be satiated until they have conceived, created and constructed an ideological ...ism.

Behind these narrow classifications of rational explanation is the quest to cast all thought into an explicable entity. They seem to think that all phenomena must be made conceptually comprehensible and coherent. It must be reduced and consolidated into an understandable unit, which can then be labeled with an ...ism. By this process of reductionism men have attempted to box up and package human thought, to nail it down in air-tight compartments, which can then be stereotyped and "pegged." Little do they seem to realize that air-tight compartments are stale, stagnant and static, chambers of death, tombs of tautology.

When the living reality and expression of the being and activity of the eternal, infinite God in His Son, Jesus Christ, is subjected to this simplification and summarization of rational explanation, He is completely diminished and transposed into a conceptual ...ism that in no way explains

188

the divine reality of Christianity. God cannot be put in a box! When men attempt to do so, they have only devised an idea of God that is no larger than their cranial cavity, and who would want a god that small? Yet, evidencing the deification of their own human reason, men have continued since the Fall to attempt to reduce God to a unit of thought. In doing so they have accepted the original temptation they that can "be like God," for they can then take the religious formulation of thought they have created in their minds, manipulate it in their own interest, and control the collective society of people thereby. Thus it is that religionism attempts to "play God" in the lives of people, and propagates a particular belief-system that becomes a distinctive ...ism of a sociological movement.

Christian Religion and its ...isms

Many are the ...isms that have formed in the context of Christian religion over the centuries, and which serve as a denial of the divine reality of Christianity. Every such ...ism serves only as a pathetic diminishment of the divine display of Christ's life in Christians. They also serve as bunkers behind which religionists can hide in order to participate in their divisive positioning and posturing,

189

instead of focusing together and being unified in the person and work of Jesus Christ.

These ...isms take different forms, so we shall consider them in five categories (which is certainly not an attempt to create an ...ism out of ...isms!). As these are very fluid, they can easily overlap and flow into one another.

(1) ...isms of ideological theories. As previously noted, many ...isms are formed as ideological constructs of thought. One of the earliest ...isms confronted by nascent Christianity was that of Greek Gnosticism, with its emphasis on the necessity of having a special knowledge of spiritual mysteries in order to advance into spiritual elitism. Though the early church rejected this philosophy, they were somewhat unaware of the extent to which the dualism of Hellenism and Platonism was affecting Christian thought. This was evidenced in an arid intellectualism and rationalism, that later led to scholasticism. The theologism of doctrinalism and creedalism soon became pervasive. Christian religion became the advocacy of a belief-system, assented to by easy-believism. This remains the focus of ideological fundamentalism and evangelicalism, defending their epistemological position with the dogmatism of

absolutism, often based on a biblicism and literalism borrowed from Judaism.

(2) ...isms of conceptual trends. Throughout the history of the Christian religion there have been philosophical and theological trends of thought that influenced the ideological theories. Behind Gnosticism there were concepts of mysticism and spiritualism, which have arisen over and over again in Christian religion. There has always been the conceptual dichotomy between the historicism that fosters conservatism and traditionalism, versus the liberalism that advocates progressivism and revolutionism. In the midst of such there has always been an expectancy of futurism, often taking variant forms of apocalypticism or millennialism, with trends toward triumphalism or pessimism. As the Christian religion adapted to its surroundings in culturalism, it often adopted new tendencies by eclecticism or syncretism. An historical review of the absorption of idealism, empiricism, pragmatism, and existentialism (just to name a few) will document the tendency to borrow the conceptual trends of humanism.

(3) ...isms of behavioral practices. The rapid rate of decline wherein the Christian religion degenerated into the

191

religionism of moralism and ethicism is astounding. How soon they abandoned reliance upon the dynamic grace of God for Christian behavior. For the most part they lapsed into the legalism of the old Pharisaism, but some opted for the hedonism of libertinism where "anything goes!". Subsequent emphases on behavioral practices included pietism, quietism, and the suppressionism of fleshly tendencies. On a collective level there have been calls for social activism, as well as pressured appeals to participate in evangelism and revivalism.

(4) ...isms of procedural patterns. In order to pass on the explanations of their belief-system, Christian religion instituted catechism instruction. Those who were the teachers participated in the authoritarianism of clericalism, and its eventual professionalism. The inevitable politicism of the church leadership resulted in hierarchicalism and papalism. As they conducted the public gatherings of the Christian religion, these same leaders encouraged ceremonialism and formalism through ritualism and liturgism. Sacramentalism further tied the participants to the procedural patterns of the priests. Though there were some Christians who attempted to escape all worldliness through asceticism or monasticism, the vast majority

accepted the proceduralisms of what would later take the forms of methodism, congregationalism, and the like.

(5) ...isms of sociological movements. As the theories, trends, practices and procedures were implemented, the collectivism of a sociological movement took place. What was to have been the collective expression of Christianity in the Church, now took the form of ecclesiasticism and institutionalism. Though the universality of Catholicism held this together in a singular sociological institution for many centuries, it was eventually severed by Protestantism, which eventually splintered into sectarianism and a diverse denominationalism, which has never unified despite the attempts of ecumenism. Theological groupings were often identified by the ideology of a particular personage, such as Augustinianism, Thomism, Lutheranism, Calvinism, Arminianism, Wesleyanism, etc. Other groups are identified by ethnicity, ex. Anglicanism, or by polity, ex. Presbyterianism.

This brief review of religious ...isms is by no means exhaustive, and could surely be multiplied many times with other examples and other categories. The intent is solely to expose the propensity to accumulate ...isms in the Christian religion.

Christianity is not an ...ism

All ...isms are antithetical to Christianity, and are
necessarily a reductionism of the spiritual reality that is
Christianity. All ...isms are an attempt to encapsulate or
encompass Christianity into an entity (be it ideological,
conceptual, behavioral, procedural or sociological) that can
in no wise contain the supernatural activity of the Living
God. The being and activity of the God of the universe will
never be confined in a bottle or box of man's making and
understanding.

Christianity is alive with the living expression of the
life of the risen Lord Jesus. Christianity is the ontological
dynamic of Jesus who is "alive and well" in Christians
today, just as in every generation since Pentecost. He
cannot be bound up in the religion of ideology, behavior,
procedures or institutions. He is free to express His divinity
in our humanity!

Whereas ...isms are fixed and unchanging in their
parameters, having been carefully clarified and defined, the
life of Jesus Christ expressed in Christians is spontaneous,
unique and creative; ever-changing and surprising – never
capable of being stereotyped and regulated. The only
pattern is the consistency of the immutable character of

Christ in the midst of the multitudinous expressions of His life in Christian behavior.

Collectively, His life is expressed in the ecclesia of the Body of Christ, the Church (Eph. 1:22,23; Col. 1:18,24). Never intended to be an organizational institution, the Church is a living spiritual organism wherein the life of Jesus Christ is expressed interactively and socially in loving interpersonal relationships. As the character of Christ's "love, joy, peace, patience, kindness, goodness,... (Gal. 5:22,23) is manifested toward one another in Christian relationships, Christianity becomes the restoration of man, both in individual behavior and in collective community.

Christianity is not an ...ism! Christianity is Christ!

Chapter Eight

CHRISTIANITY IS *NOT* PROBLEM-SOLVING

In raised gold letters over the ornate entrance, the sign read "Global Repair and Rehabilitation Enterprises." The corporate offices of this successful worldwide business were topped with a spire, and the windows were formed of stained-glass designed by the world's best artisans. The founder of this enterprise, Mr. J. C. Soterion, was known throughout the business world as "Mr. Fix-it." His hand-picked successors had built up the business with the stated objective to fix, correct and solve every problem known to man. By aggressive marketing and multinational franchising the incorporation was eventually able to engage in corporate diversification that allowed for specialization in every area of problem-solving. By the further development of political alliances with "the powers that be" throughout the world, this institution was engaged in every feasible solution to relieve, resolve and remedy the needs and problems of mankind.

This tongue-in-cheek parody obviously portrays Christian religion and the institutional church as a business enterprise dedicated to solving all the problems of the world. Has not Christendom often projected this to be the objective of its religious business? Perhaps it is time to question and evaluate the legitimate objectives of Christianity.

At the outset, one must admit that there are "a million and one," i.e. innumerable, needs and problems in the world today. In the fallen world-order of depraved humanity and the consequent corruption and perversion of all social structures and institutions, the needs and problems are never-ending. They go with the territory. They are part and parcel of the problematic nemesis brought on by the introduction of sin in the human race.

The question is, though, "What can be done to resolve these needs and problems of mankind?" Can mankind, individually or collectively, find solutions and remedies to rectify the situation? Do Christians have any responsibility to attempt to deliver and "save" the fallen world-system from their problems? Jacques Ellul, French sociologist, historian of social institutions, professor of law, and an active Christian leader in the Reformed Church of France, asks the question thusly,

> "Who tells us anyway that all human problems should or can be solved? Perhaps unsolved problems are more important for God than solutions are...since they remind us of man's sin and the divine redemption. Perhaps man's problems are so complicated and so badly put that they are in fact insoluble. The problem of wealth and poverty will never be solved except as it remains unsolved. The organized battle of the Church against temporal evils like slavery, intemperance, and national division runs into the same difficulties as the Crusades. Its experience gives us good reason to ask to what extent it is the church's mission to solve these temporal problems."[1]

It is certainly legitimate to question whether it is the task of Christians to attempt to solve problems within the arena of the fallen world-order.

The story of Daniel and King Belshazzar, recorded in the fifth chapter of Daniel (5:1-31), seems to set the stage for a consideration of whether we have any responsibility to engage in problem-solving in the context of the world-system. King Belshazzar, son of King Nebuchadnezzar, while in the midst of idolatrous carousing saw some handwriting on the wall. Disturbed by what he saw, he determined to seek an alliance with religion to interpret and solve the problem (a mutually expedient alliance

199

throughout human history). Eventually Daniel the prophet was summoned to interpret the situation, be an "answer man," and "solve difficult problems" (cf. Dan. 5:12,16). King Belshazzar offered to reward and remunerate Daniel, to praise and promote him, but Daniel was not interested in the baubles and benefits of engaging in religio-political problem-solving, and told the King to "keep his gifts." Daniel was willing, however, to proclaim what God had revealed to him, and forthwith told the King that his life and kingdom was full of sin, didn't add up to the character of God, and would soon be decimated and brought to an end. That very night King Belshazzar was slain, and his kingdom was divided among the Medes and the Persians. Is there a "message" here that warns against the mutually expedient alliances that would seek to interpret, answer and "solve the difficult problems" of the world? Should Christians, likewise, be making a proclamation of the revelation of God in Jesus Christ, which explains that He has "overcome the world" (John 16:33), that "the ruler of this world has been judged" (John 16:11), and "shall be cast out" (John 12:31)?

If we look at the life, ministry and redemptive efficacy of Jesus Christ perhaps we shall see even more clearly the pattern of approach to the world and its problems that Christians should have. British Bible teacher, Maj. W. Ian Thomas notes that

> "the Lord Jesus Christ refused to be committed to the parochial needs of His own day and generation; He was not committed to the political situation in Palestine, or to the emancipation of the Jewish nation from the Roman yoke! He was not committed to the pressing social problems of His time, nor to one faction as opposed to another, any more than today He is committed to the West against the East, or to the Republicans against the Democrats (as though either were less wicked than the other!). Christ was not even committed to the needs of a perishing world; He was neither unmindful nor unmoved by all these other issues, but as Perfect Man He was committed to His Father, and for that only to which His Father was committed in Him – exclusively!"[2]

Despite the incessant religious calls to respond to the "needs" of the world, and to dedicate and commit ourselves to solve the physical, psychological and spiritual problems of mankind, it does not appear that these guilt-producing obligations are consistent with Christian responsibility. Rather than being religiously committed to responding to and solving the problems of the world, we are to be submitted (cf. James 4:7) to whatever God in Christ is committed to being and doing in us. What a relief and release from the performance-oriented burden of religious obligation! In the obedience of "listening under" (*hupakouo*) the direction and leading of the Spirit of Christ

201

(cf. Rom. 8:14), we live and act by the grace-dynamic of God as He leads and empowers genuine Christian ministry.

Some have attempted to portray Jesus as a political and religious revolutionary-activist. Such actions as overturning the tables in the temple and standing up to the religious and secular authorities can easily be misconstrued as having such motivation, but a larger perspective of Jesus' ministry does not lend itself to the support of such an agenda. His intent was indeed revolutionary, but not in the sense of political insurrection or social transformation, but rather in a radically different concept of "kingdom" wherein He as the divine king would reign and rule as Lord in the lives of the people of God, manifesting His character which is diametrically opposite of that evidenced in the fallen world-order. Indeed, there was a predicament or problem to solve in order to effect such a kingdom – the alienation of man from God by his spiritual condition and behavioral expression of sin. In an act that accepted the appearance of powerlessness and weakness, Jesus voluntarily submitted in obedience (cf. Phil. 2:8) to vicariously and substitutionally take the consequences of humanity's sin in death. In this remedial action of redemption He would take the death consequences of our sin, in order that the reality of His divine life might be restored to mankind. From the cross He exclaimed, *"Tetelestai!"* "It is finished!" "Problem solved!" (John 19:30). Inexorably setting in motion the entire restorational objective of restoring God's life to man, Jesus knew that the resurrection, Pentecostal outpouring and consummatory glorification were assured. In this "finished work" of Jesus Christ, God graciously solved the ultimate problem of mankind.

When Christian religion reverts to secondary efforts of problem-solving as their primary mission in the world, they are in effect denying the "finished work" of Christ by focusing on and engaging in "works" that attempt to "finish" God's work on His behalf, instead of relying on what has been accomplished once and for all mankind in Christ. Yet, Christian religion has often projected itself as the "force of good" to change or transform the world of evil, perceiving its role in a "savior-complex" that sets out to deliver the world from its problems. Robert Capon's remarks are pertinent:

> "Christianity is not a religion. Christianity is the proclamation of the end of religion, not of a new religion, or even of the best of all religions. ...If the cross is the sign of anything, it's the sign that God has gone out of the religion business and solved all of the world's problems without requiring a single human being to do a single religious thing. What the cross is actually a sign of is the

> fact that religion can't do a thing about the world's problems – that
> it never did work and it never will..."₃

Failing to recognize the grace of God in Jesus Christ, Christian religion marches on to garner its forces for a particular *cause celebre* in order to create a social movement to attempt to fix the ills and woes of the world. Rather than explaining the victory won by Christ over all evil, they seek to expunge the perceived evils in the world, often by socio-political and religious reform movements that offer a pseudo-salvation. This is ever so close to the Marxist objectives to "change the world" through socio-economic transformation. Commenting on this tendency of Christian religion to become involved in socio-political transformationism, that he terms "the false presence of the kingdom" in a book so entitled, Jacques Ellul observes that

> "every time the Church has gotten into the political game, no
> matter what the manner of her entry, no matter what her opinion or
> opposing choices in a political situation with regard to an
> institution, she has been drawn every time into a betrayal, either of
> revealed truth or of the incarnate love. She has become involved
> every time in apostasy. ...Politics is the Church's worst problem. It
> is her constant temptation, the occasion of her greatest disasters,
> the trap continually set for her by the Prince of this world."₄

When religion engages in social problem-solving, especially in alliance with the secular governmental structures which have succumbed to the evil of fallen men and thus designated as opposing "principalities and powers' (cf. Eph. 6:12), then it has joined the action on the devil's playground. They participate in the diabolic power-struggles of human social pyramids. To be sure, there is a place for such social problem-solving. Secular governments are obliged to engage in such. Religion will inevitably advocate such. Genuine Christianity does not seek to eliminate, destroy or debunk such involvement by these human institutions, but only to devalue such by recognizing that it is not an end in itself, and will not ultimately solve the world's problems. All the while Christians must recognize that peripheral problem-solving in the arena of the fallen world-order is not the primary task or mission of the church, and that there is no particular "Christian solution" for every perceived problem in the world.

Problem-solving religion becomes but another social agent utilizing expedient tools of force as clubs by justifying the "might of the right" and the "right of might" in the power-plays of the world arena. Playing the world's game by using their methodology, such religion does not help the situation, but becomes part of the problem in their self-effort to provide remedies. When Christians think that they are "serving" God by attempting to solve the problems of people and the world, they fail to understand that "God is not served with human hands" (Acts 17:25) and their attempts to help God out in problem-solving is not helpful. Human helpfulness is not helpful from God's perspective. If it is not His activity, done His way by Him, then it is not worth doing. In addition, problem-solving religion is impatient in its desires to achieve its objectives. It wants to perform, attack, assault, seize the day as it engages in its agenda of activistic resolution. Waiting upon God and allowing Him in His sovereignty to deal with life and the world in His time and in His way can only be conceived as passivistic acquiescence by those who view the Christian purpose as problem-solving.

Christians have failed to understand the reality of the "good news" they proclaim. Christianity is not a premise, proposition, program or procedure to be applied to the problems of the fallen world. What we have to share is not a magic potion; an elixir that makes everything turn out right. The gospel is not a panacea, a cure-all, a remedy for all ills. It is not a "philosopher's stone" that conjures up some imaginary spiritual substance that will turn the base metals of society into utopian gold, as the catholicon of the world's woes. The "good news" of Christianity is the living

Person of Jesus Christ, rather than a packaged solution to an identifiable social or personal problem. Even if the perceived problem is the spiritual depravity of an unregenerate individual, we do not extend or apply a packaged salvation to fix their spiritual problem, but point them to, and seek to introduce them to the risen Lord Jesus as their Savior. And even this mission objective must not be perceived as a problem-solving project to win the world to Christ by a particular point in time. Christianity is not a problem-solving project to create perfect individuals, perfect churches, a perfect society, or a perfect world. Rather, Christianity is a personal Savior, Jesus Christ. He did not come to be a remedy to problems, but to be the Redeemer of mankind.

When Christianity is regarded as a packaged solution to identifiable social or personal problems, the reality of Christianity becomes objectified as an "it," some "thing" to be applied to a problem as a utilitarian instrument. The message of Christianity is thus static and objectified, linear and causal, historicized and theologized as a personal and social solution. Jesus is not a solution! He is "the way, the truth and the life" (John 14:6), the modality, reality and vitality of God who has invested Himself into the human condition and situation. He is the ontological Being who activates His creation.

We must recognize that there will always be problems in this fallen world-order. They are intrinsic to the character of the Evil One, the "god of this world" (II Cor. 4:4), as he causes and creates his character to be energized in the individuals (cf. Eph. 2:2) and social structures of the world-order of evil. The Scriptures do not "sugar-coat" the situation for the Christian who is "in the world, but not of the world" (cf. John 17:11,14). Poverty is perennially present (cf. Matt. 26:11). We are promised tribulation (John 16:33) and "difficult times" (II Tim. 3:1). It seems that one of the greatest temptations among Christian peoples is to aspire to be free of any problems here on earth. Lloyd Ogilvie explains that

> "the greatest problem we all share, to a greater or lesser degree, is a profound misunderstanding of the positive purpose of problems. Until we grapple with this gigantic problem, we will be helpless victims of our problems all through our lives."[5]

Tim Hansel amplifies this theme by noting that

> "most people think of problems as something bad, as some terrible interruption in their lives which they wish they did not have to endure. In truth, problems in and of themselves are not necessarily bad. It is interesting to note that the actual Greek root of the word 'problem,' namely, *probalein*, means to throw or to thrust forward.

208

> Problems are the very means by which God drives us forward. Without problems, there would be no growth."[6]

Although these authors are addressing personal problems of the individual instead of the general problems of the world, the common thread is the necessity of accepting problems. In fact, Thomas Merton comments that "a life without problems is hopeless." Biblical hope is the confident expectation that things will be better than they presently are. Those who yearn for a life without problems – the esoteric mystic and the social liberal both seem to share this unachievable objective – thus yearn for an overly-realized eschatological situation absent of hope.

Until the consummation of the grand experiment of humanity on earth, when Christ shall return and there will be a "new heaven and a new earth" (II Pet. 3:13), we can expect personal and social problems. To think that Christians are going to solve all the problems of the world is akin to thinking that a forest fire engulfing our planet could be quenched by Christians collectively beating back the flames with their Bibles. It is all going to burn up eventually, and the fires of hell are not going to be quenched.

In the meantime we must recognize that the presence of the Christian kingdom in the context of the fallen world of evil, instead of solving all problems, creates a whole new set of problems. The anomalous reality of kingdom-living in the world exposes, subverts, and upsets the *modus operandi* of the world-system. That is why Jesus warned that His presence would bring the family dissension of "brother against brother" (Matt. 10:35), and the conflict of a "sword" (Matt. 10:35). Christian reality, being antithetical to the world's ways, creates but another insurmountable problem for the world-order as it seeks to solve the world's problems.

We must not leave the impression that Christianity necessarily advocates a passivistic acceptance of the status-quo; that it is unconcerned about the world situation in a retreat from cultural relevance. Nothing could be farther from the truth. The love, mercy, and compassion of God in the Christian seeks the highest good of suffering mankind. Evangelism, social action, political involvement, relief efforts are all legitimate, as long as we realistically realize that we cannot and will not solve all the problems of the world; and we will not produce a perfectionistic, problem-free utopian existence here on earth. Misguided religious efforts to manipulate such results through man-made techniques and timetables, only reveal that religious man is still attempting to set himself up as God to "play Holy Spirit," without reckoning on God's grace-action in His due time.

An historical example of God's timely action apart from religious orchestration might be the effect that Christianity has had upon slavery. Human slavery had been a social ill throughout human history, but

> "neither Jesus nor the apostles thought they could solve the problem of slavery as a social problem. They did not revolt against the practice. They did not contend for the dignity of the human person. They did not attempt institutional transformation. The first Christians were content to adopt an individual relation to slaves which changed the situation from within. This is what finally brought about, after many centuries, the abolition of slavery."[7]

Slaves were encouraged to obey their masters as "unto the Lord", and masters were encouraged to treat their slaves with loving kindness, fairness and justice (Eph. 6:5-9; Col. 3:22-4:1). The tragic situation of human slavery was gradually diminished as the character of Christ was expressed in the midst of the problem. Such is the revolutionary permeation of "salt" and "light" into the world (cf. Matt. 5:13-16).

Christianity is not problem-solving! Christianity is Christ! Christianity is the ontological dynamic of the divine life of the risen Lord Jesus lived out in the active behavior of receptive Christians, and that within the perplexities of a plethora of personal, social, and world problems. Christianity is Christ's life lived out in Christians in every context of clashing cultures, differing ideologies, and pluralistic perspectives. Such manifestation of Christ's life (cf. II Cor. 4:10,11) may resolve some perceived problems among men, but problem-solving is not the mission objective of Christianity.

The teleological purpose of Christianity is not utilitarian solutions to perceived problems, but receptivity to the ontological character of God expressed in behavior that glorifies God. We are "created for His glory" (Isa. 43:7). God does not give His glory to another (cf. Isa. 42:8; 48:11) in the form of accolades and "atta-boys" for the results of man-made resolutions and transformations of the world's problems. God is glorified only as His all-glorious character is lived out by the ontological dynamic of the presence, person and power of Jesus Christ by His Spirit.

Our Christian responsibility is to be available and receptive to what God in Christ wants to be and do in us.

212

By the "obedience of faith" (cf. Rom. 1:5; 16:26) we remain receptive to His activity; submitted to whatever God is committed to in us; blooming where we are planted by bearing the fruit of His character (cf. John 15:5; Gal. 5:22,23). Nothing is so contrary to our natural human tendencies, even as Christians, as the acceptance of such powerlessness, weakness, inability and inadequacy that must rely on God's action of grace in all behavior and action. Every tenet of the fallen humanistic perspective posits human productivity and activity as the causal element of the betterment of mankind, so for the Christian to accept the radical *modus operandi* of faithful receptivity of divine activity in what by all appearances seems to be inutility and uselessness$_8$ is diametrically different than the way the world operates. Jesus was so right when He said, "My kingdom is not of this world" (John 18:36).

In explaining *The Presence of the Kingdom*, Jacques Ellul writes:

> "Our world is entirely directed towards action. Everything is interpreted in terms of action. People are always looking for slogans, programmes, ways of action; action for action's sake. Our world is so obsessed by activity that it is in danger of losing its life. A man who spends all his time in action, by that very fact ceases to live.
> The world only desires action, and has no desire for life at all. ...What matters is to live, and not to act. ...What we need to do is to

live, and to refuse to accept the methods of action proposed by the world,...(even) the church's 'calls to action' made in miserable imitation of the world.

Men should be alive, instead of being obsessed with action. To be alive means the total situation of man as he is confronted by God...living to the glory of the Creator."9

Ponder the succinct statement that Ellul makes: "A man who spends all his time in action, by that very fact ceases to live." That is worthy of repeated contemplation. When Christians spend all their time in activistic problem-solving, they cease to live abundantly (cf. John 10:10) as Christ intends. The objective of Christianity is to allow for the ontological Being of the Life of God in Christ to be expressed in the character of our behavior unto the glory of God, rather than to engage in humanly conceived and executed utilitarian actions and religious endeavors.

What, then, is the active responsibility of the Christian individual? We actively make the choice of faith to be receptive and available to all that God wants to be and do in us by the grace-dynamic of the Person and work of Jesus Christ. In obedience we "listen under" the guidance and direction of God's Spirit to discern His course of action; how He desires to enact His Being in our behavior. "He who began a good work in you, will perfect it until the day of Christ Jesus" (Phil. 1:6). Herein is the freedom from the performance of problem-solving programs; the individual freedom to be man as God intended man to be. Once again Ellul so aptly notes:

> "There are no clear, simple, universal, Christian solutions to all the problems which arise. We can only put the problems as clearly as possible and then, having given the believer all the weapons that theology and piety can offer, say to him: 'Now it is up to you to go and find the answer, not intellectually, but by living out your faith in this situation.' There is no prefabricated solution nor universally applicable model of Christian life. ...Freedom implies that each Christian discovers for himself the style and form of his action."[10]

In the freedom of faithful receptivity, we the Christian kingdom-community, individually and collectively, allow for the radical and revolutionary life of Jesus Christ to be incarnated and manifested in our mortal flesh (cf. II Cor. 4:10,11) by the Holy Spirit.

Problems will inevitably present themselves in the midst of the fallen world-order (and perhaps intensify) until the end of time. Christians should not expect to solve the world's problems. Living, as we do, in the enigma of the interim between Christ's "finished work" in the crucifixion and resurrection, and the consummation of that victory upon His return, the problems of the world may seem to be overwhelming, but we live in the confident expectation of hope that all will be resolved in the final casting out of evil

215

and its problems, and the restoration of creation in "the new heaven and new earth."

Christianity is not problem-solving! Christianity is the life of Jesus Christ lived out in the midst of present problems, evidencing His sufficiency in all situations.

Chapter Nine

CHRISTIANITY IS *NOT* AN IDEOLOGICAL OPTION

The Issue is Life or Death

Those outside of the Christian faith often view Christianity as but an ideological option among many such religious and philosophical options available to human reasoning, acceptance, or devotion. As they pass by the smorgasbord of human thought, many people believe that the objective is to select one, or perhaps a combination of many ideas, that they find preferable or palatable to suit their personal tastes. Having done so, they can then settle-in to a contented enjoyment of their belief choices, and advocate that others do the same.

Christians are partly to blame for this skewed perspective of Christianity as an ideological option. Christians have often projected the idea that Christianity is a "believe-right religion" – an epistemological exercise in developing a belief-system that aligns with correct historical interpretation, orthodox theological formulation, and accurate doctrines carefully worded in a creedal "statement of faith." The "believe-right religion" then becomes a "do-right religion," as moral standards and ethical guidelines are formulated to correspond with the ideological beliefs, and to enforce behavioral conformity "in deed and word."

It is time to recognize and assert, "Christianity is not an ideological option." Mankind is not faced with a multiple-choice quiz wherein an individual must pick and choose one of several ideas to the exclusion of all others, or "all of the above" in an inclusive combination of belief tenets. Though the human race is indeed confronted with a plurality of ideological options competing for acceptance in men's minds, the Christian gospel is not one of those ideological options. Conservative, fundamentalistic Christian religion may project that Christianity is a superior ideological option that excludes all other options as inferior, fallacious and unbelievable, thus justifying their attempts to conserve their own belief as the only viable option of fundamental faith. Liberal and progressive

Christian religion, on the other hand, may depict Christianity as an ideological option among a plurality of belief-options of equivalent veracity and validity, allowing the individual to choose one option, or a combination of several, or to inclusively incorporate all options as but differing paths by which to approach the one god of the universe. Both of these approaches, the fundamentalist that seeks to establish an absolutist belief statement that excludes all others, and the liberal that allows an inclusive eclecticism that merges all thought into relativism, mistakenly view the Christian gospel as an ideological option. The issue that the Christian gospel confronts us with is not a choice of an ideological option, but the choice of life or death.

Allow me to illustrate in the form of an analogy, admitting at the outset that the correspondences in all analogies "break down" sooner or later. The reader will soon detect that the details of this analogy have their "breaking point."

A certain man (isn't that how Jesus started many of His parabolic analogies?) made an appointment with his family physician to find out if the doctor could diagnose some health problems he was experiencing.

"What are your symptoms?" the doctor asked.

"Doc, I am experiencing pain in this region of my body, and I have noticed some discharges which I did not previously have," the man responded.

The physician examined the man, conducted an array of medical tests, and sent some specimens to the medical laboratory for analysis. When the results of the lab tests were available, the physician consulted with his patient and advised him that the reports indicated there were some physical abnormalities that would best be treated by a medical specialist. "I am referring you to a specialist in this field of medicine," the doctor intoned.

The medical specialist conducted more comprehensive biological tests, and sent additional specimens to the laboratory. When these lab tests were returned, the specialist consulted with the man, and compassionately reported the diagnosis to him. "You have a form of cancer," the doctor explained, and this kind of cancer can be terminal. It can result in death."

"What are my options?" the man asked.

"If left untreated, you will die in the near future," the doctor replied. "The only other option is a singular treatment regimen available for this particular kind of cancer. But I must advise you that the treatment is not easy or pleasant. In fact, it is painful and uncomfortable. It requires responsibility on the part of the patient to stay with the regimen of the treatment, and will require the curtailment of some of your scheduled activities. But this treatment has proven quite successful for this form of cancer, and will probably allow you to live a prolonged life" (though not "eternal", for this is where the analogy breaks down!). "It is your choice," the doctor explained, "and I recognize that such decisions can be difficult. I will not pressure, manipulate or coerce your choice."

The man responded to the doctor somewhat indignantly. "Well, I do not like those options, doctor. It does not seem fair to me that this should be my only choice. It seems to me to be exclusivistic, and I do not appreciate exclusivism."

The doctor, taken aback by such a response, replied, "Well, I don't understand why you think this is exclusivism. To exclude is to 'cut out." You are not

221

being 'cut out' or 'shut out.' You are being given an option, an either-or choice of treatment or the rejection of treatment. But it does come down to a choice of life or death. Do nothing about the cancer that has invaded you body, and you will die. Accept and receive the only known treatment for this kind of cancer, along with its accompanying side-effects, and you will live (longer). The only 'exclusion' here is that you will 'exclude' yourself from *life*, and consign yourself to *death*, if you refuse the singular treatment available to you. But, that is *your* choice!"

The correspondence of this analogy to the availability of life in Jesus Christ through the Christian gospel is self-evident, but allow me to make some observations.

The "natural man" (cf. I Cor. 2:14) wants a plurality of options, whether it is medical treatments or ideological beliefs. Why is this so? Because the "natural man" views himself in the elevated position of being an autonomous arbiter, freely choosing what he determines to be the best option. Having deified human reason in his own cognitive abilities and opinions, the humanistic rationalism of fallen man insists on a "multiple-choice" from among a plurality of options. Thus he can "play God" in making the choice of "acceptable" or "unacceptable." If a singular either-or choice is presented, this "wisdom of the world" (I Cor. 1:20) inevitably complains of "exclusivism",

Singularity of solution does not of necessity imply exclusivism. Do we complain to the scientific physicist of cosmology, "I cannot/will not accept the singularity of your 'Big Bang theory' of cosmological origins, because it is exclusivistic"? "I demand a spectrum of options from which to choose, or perhaps to form my own eclectic amalgam of opinions." No, for singularity does not imply exclusivism.

The message of the Christian gospel is that the singular God ("God is one" – Deut. 6:4) sent His singular ("only begotten" – John 3:16,18; I John 4:9) Son on a singular redemptive mission (cf. Jude 1:3) to earth in incarnational identification with man (cf. John 1:14; Phil. 2:6-8). The Son offered up Himself (cf. Gal. 2:20; Heb. 7:27) as the singular ("once and for all" – Rom. 6:10; Heb. 10:12) sacrifice to take upon Himself the death consequences of man's sin, and make His singular eternal life (cf. I John 5:12,13) available to all mankind. That is why Jesus says, 'I AM the way, the truth, and the life; no man comes to the

Father but through Me" (John 14:6). This is not exclusivism; but it is a singularity of life option. "There is no other name given among men by which a man must be saved" (Acts 4:12), declared Peter in the first sermon of the church. No one is excluded or "cut out," for all men universally, without discrimination, are invited to make the either-or decision to receive Christ's life. "God is not willing that any should perish, but that all may come to repentance" (II Pet. 3:9). "Whoever will call upon the Lord will be saved" (Rom. 10:13).

Jesus did not say, "I came that you might have ideological options presented to your human reasoning with the assumed autonomous ability to accept, reject, or merge these in exclusivism or inclusivism, and thus to be contented with your choice." What He did say was, "I came that you might have life, and have it more abundantly" (John 10:10). "I am that life" (John 14:6). "He who believes in the Son has eternal life, but he who does not obey the Son shall not see life" (John 3:36). "He who believes in Me shall never die" (John 11:26), i.e. shall not experience the "second death" (cf. Rev. 2:11; 20:14). The issue is life or death! "The wages of sin is death, but the

free gift of God is eternal life in Christ Jesus our Lord"
(Rom. 6:23).

The charge of "exclusivism" is only made by those who
improperly consider Christianity to be an ideological option
among a multiplicity of ideological options offered by men
(not God) through the centuries. Such a charge of
"exclusivism" will inevitably and always be made by those
who refuse to accept Jesus Christ as the only "life option,"
the singular solution to the sin problem, and the singular
source of salvation that restores mankind to God's intent.
Unbelievers always demand other options so they can
employ their deified human reasoning to be the final judge
of what is acceptable or unacceptable, right or wrong, life
or death. They want to "play God." Concurrent with their
charges of "exclusivism", they will always argue for an
inclusivity that gives equal credence to all belief-constructs
or ideological options, claiming that all roads lead to the
same religious reality with variant expressions. This always
leads to relativism, allowing every individual to construct
their own truth, and declaring truth to be whatever they
perceive it to be. Again, setting themselves up as God.

The Christian gospel is not an ideological option
alongside many others. Rather, the Christian gospel is the

good news of the singular source of spiritual life in Jesus Christ, in contrast to spiritual death presently and in the hereafter. Exclusivity or inclusivity of ideological options is not the issue. The issue is life or death! Mankind has been offered an either-or, "Yes" or "No" choice of whether we will accept spiritual and eternal life in Christ, or reject Him. "He who has the Son has life; he who does not have the Son of God does not have life" (I John 5:12).

The only "exclusion" is that an individual will "exclude" himself from *life*, and consign himself to *death*, if he refuses to accept and receive the singular treatment option that is available in Jesus Christ. But that is his choice!

Chapter Ten

CHRISTIANITY IS CHRIST

There will be some who will think that we have
belabored the point in explaining what Christianity is *not*!
Explanation by negation was necessary, particularly
because of the contemporary confusion that melds
Christianity with religion and all of its expressions.
Although we have alluded in all of the previous chapters to
the reality of Christianity in the living dynamic of Jesus
Christ, we shall now set forth a positive expression of the
fact that "Christianity is Christ."

What does it mean to be a Christian?

What is Christianity?

Confusion over the meaning of these terms, and
misunderstanding of the reality implied by these terms, has
resulted in gross misrepresentations of the same, even by
those who would claim to be Christians engaged in

Christianity. It is, therefore, of utmost importance that we re-evaluate the reality of Christianity.

Followers of Jesus were "first called Christians in Antioch" (Acts 11:26). Perhaps it was initially a label of derision or derogation, but King Agrippa seems to have used the term as a neutral designation of one believing in Jesus Christ (Acts 26:28), and Peter employs it as an accepted reference to those identified with the name of Christ (I Peter 4:16). Immediately thereafter the over-all phenomenon of persons identifying with Jesus Christ was generalized as "Christianity." Ignatius and Polycarp, disciples of the apostle John, used the Greek word *christianismos* in the late first or early second century, and later writers used the Latin word *christianitas*.

Semantic variations of meaning have proliferated through the centuries unto the present. The term "Christianity" has been used to designate one of the world's religions. It is analyzed historically as the events of its adherents and institutions through the centuries of almost two millennia. "Christianity" is often used synonymously with "Christendom," although the latter term is often used pejoratively of institutionalized Christian religion. In his *Attack on Christendom*, Kierkegaard complained that everyone in Denmark considered themselves to be "Christians" because they were born into the state church and baptized as infants, concluding that "if everyone is a Christian, then no one is a Christian." Witch-hunts, inquisitions and political wars have been conducted in the name of "Christian religion." Many have subsequently rejected "Christianity," offended or injured by its multitudinous religious aberrations and injustices. Still others (as we shall do in this study), reserve the term "Christianity" for the spiritual reality of the function of the living Lord Jesus in Christians.

The mere usage of terminology is not our objective, though, since language is in constant flux. Rather, the questions are: What was the initial and Biblical understanding of what it meant to be a Christian? What do the Biblical writers imply to be the essence of Christianity?

Although the term "Christianity" is not found in the Scriptures, we will consider it to be indicative of everything that Jesus Christ came to be and to do. The entirety of the revelation of God to man is constituted and comprised of the person and work of Jesus Christ. In and by His Son, God enacted everything necessary to restore mankind to His divinely intended function, reinvesting man with the spiritual reality of the presence and function of deity within humanity. When Jesus thus dwells and reigns spiritually in those who receive Him by faith, the kingdom that Jesus so often referred to becomes operative. The resurrection-life of Jesus becomes the spiritual empowering of the Christian's life and participation in the ecclesia of the Church. Such a spiritual, gospel reality of "Christianity" can only be defined as the dynamic life and activity of the living Lord Jesus Christ. Christianity is Christ!

C.S. Lewis explained that

"in Christ a new kind of man appeared: and the new kind of life which began in Him is to be ut into us."[1]

Earlier John W. Nevin had written,

"A new order of revelation entirely bursts upon the world, in the person of Jesus Christ. He is the absolute truth itself, personally present among men, and incorporating itself with their life. He is the substance, where all previous prophecy, had been only as sound or shadow."[2]

God's self-revelation of Himself in His Son, Jesus Christ, involves an integral and indivisible oneness. The singular unity of the Godhead Self-communicates Himself to man in the *homoousion* union of Father, Son and Holy Spirit. In this divine triunity there can be no bifurcation or trifurcation of independent function. God acts as unified oneness. When he acts He does what He does because He is who He is. His Being is expressed in His activity, and His activity is always expressive of His Being. He never acts "out of character." His actions are never detached from the manifestation of who He is in Himself; they are never static, disconnected actions separated or severed from the expression of His Being. All that God has to give is a self-giving of Himself – His Being in action. He does not reveal or offer some "thing" about Himself. He cannot be thus parted or sectioned. Nor does He extend some commodity or product distinct from Himself. God reveals Himself and acts in grace (John 1:17) by the power of the Spirit in His Son, Jesus Christ. "No one knows who the Son is except the Father, and who the Father is except the Son, and anyone to whom the Son will to reveal Himself" (Lk. 10:22). The self-revelation of God in the Messianic Son must always be understood in their essential oneness of divine Being, as well as the integral unity of their Being and action. God reveals Himself in the Son. He gives Himself to man. Jesus Christ reveals the gospel in Himself. He gives Himself to man as God.

Dualistic Detachment

The failure to maintain the unity of the Father, Son and Holy Spirit in the unity of their Being and action always leads to aberrational understandings and expressions of Christianity. The history of Christian religion (as distinct from Christianity) is replete with man's attempts to divide the persons of the Godhead into distinct functions, and to sever Christ's work from His person. This latter disjunctive dualism is the more subtle and the most prevalent throughout what is called "Christian history." Christianity is conceived of as some "thing" established apart from, and distinct from, Christ Himself. The gospel, the Church, the kingdom are regarded as separate entities offered, extended, established, effected or dispensed by Jesus Christ, independent of Himself. T.F. Torrance correctly identifies such "detachment of Christianity from Christ",[3] as the result of epistemological dualism, noting that

> "fundamentalism is unwilling to acknowledge the identity in being between what God is toward us in His revelation in Jesus Christ and what He is in His living Being and Reality in Himself."[4]

Examples of such "separated concepts" of fundamentalist dualism should be instructive, if not convicting:

232

The historical Jesus is often remembered as the historical founder of a religion, the history of which can be documented and analyzed. The life of Jesus on earth, and the specific events thereof, are memorialized. The story is borne from generation to generation in special commemorations: "Happy Birthday Jesus" (Christmas) and "Remember the Resurrection" (Easter). How does this differ from the celebratory remembrances of George Washington's Birthday and the call to "Remember Pearl Harbor"? When Christianity is falsely conceived of as an historical society for the memory of and/or worship of an historically detached founder, there is a disjunctive dualism between Jesus Christ and what is called "Christianity."

When Jesus is portrayed as merely a religious or theological teacher, then the content of His teaching becomes an ideological belief-system distinct from His person. Even when Jesus is correctly identified as the mediatorial representative of God (I Tim. 2:5), the High Priest of God (Heb. 3:1; 8:1), the Son of God (John 11:27), the rational formulation of doctrinal and theological propositions can be formed into systematized constructs of interpretation that stand alone from the living presence of Jesus Christ. Christianity then becomes a theological

233

society for the explanation of and debate of theological truths in propositional and sentential precision, with no reception and experience of the person of the risen Lord Jesus.

Jesus can be proclaimed as the Savior of mankind, as He is within evangelical preaching, but when the Savior is detached from the process of salvation a transactional dualism results. If Jesus is but the benefactor of the benefits of salvation, then He is but the source of commodities, "goods," services, products or possessions that are dispensed, conferred or endowed by one who is dualistically distinct from that which is delivered. The spiritual Deliverer becomes but a religious dispenser.

Those that advocate a behavioristic morality or "Christian ethic" that divorces the doing of good from the dynamic of the God-man, Jesus Christ, create a disconnected dualism that encourages and expects behavior that conforms to the codified rules and regulations by means of employing procedures, techniques and behavioral formulas, rather than deriving divine character, the "fruit of the Spirit" (Gal. 5:22,23), from the Spirit of Christ (Rom. 8:9). Such moral "works" may be enacted for personal spirituality or for the social good and betterment of mankind at large, but when engaged in apart from the outworking of Christ's life, they remain disengaged from the reality of Christianity.

A fragmented dualism also results when Jesus Christ is not held in organic union with the Church, the Body of Christ. Jesus is not the "Head of the Church" only in terms of being an hierarchical head of an organizational institution. Neither is He the "head" in the sense of being the fountainhead and founder of a religion that bears His name. His headship is not merely instrumental in the establishment of a corporate ecclesiasticism that would serve as the depository, conservatory and dispensary of grace and truth, as if these could be dissected from the divine action of God in Christ.

Protestantism is particularly guilty of the disassociative dualism that transfers the expressive agency of the Word of God from Jesus Christ (John 1:1,14) to the impersonalized instruction of God in an inspired book. Engaging in the biblicism of devotion to a canonical formulation, and employing various forms of interpretation, Protestant fundamentalists have developed a book-religion that often deifies the book in Bibliolatry.

William Barclay notes that,

"There was one mistake into which the early Church was never in any danger of falling. In those early days men never thought of Jesus Christ as a figure in a book. They never thought of Him as someone who had lived and died, and whose story was told and passed down in history, as the story of someone who had lived and whose life had ended. They did not think of Him as someone who had been but as someone who is. They did not think of Jesus Christ as someone whose teaching must be discussed and debated and argued about; they thought of Him as someone whose presence could be enjoyed and whose constant fellowship could be experienced. Their faith was not founded on a book; their faith was founded on a person."[5]

In accord with that opinion, Juan Carlos Ortiz writes,

"We need a new generation of Christians who know that the church is centered around a Person who lives within them. Jesus didn't leave us with just a book and tell us, 'I leave the Bible. Try to find out all you can from it by making concordances and commentaries.' No, He didn't say that. 'Lo, I am with you always,' He promised. 'I'm not leaving you with a book alone. I am there, in your hearts.' ...We just have to know that we have the Author of the book within us..."[6]

In addition to the above dualistic tendencies, we might also cite the theological dualism that has been invasive throughout the centuries of "Christian theology" in the propensity to objectify the work of Christ into external categories unattached to the personal presence of Christ by His Spirit in the Christian. When the work of Jesus is cast into legal, forensic and judicial categories that posit the transference of penalty that issues forth in the declaration and imputation of justification in the heavenly courtroom, apart from the spiritual and experiential presence of the Righteous One, Jesus Christ (I John 2:1), making us righteous (II Cor. 5:21) and manifesting the character "fruit of righteousness" (Phil. 1:11) in our behavior, we have once again divorced theology from the dynamic divine Being of the God-man, making it less that "Christian theology."

B.F. Westcott advised over a century ago:

"According to some the essence of Christianity lies in the fact that it is the supreme moral law. According to others its essence is to be found in true doctrine, or more specially in the scheme of redemption, or in the means of the union of man with God. Christianity does in fact include Law, and Doctrine, and Redemption, and Union, but it combines them all in a still wider idea. It establishes the principle of a Law, which is internal and not external, which includes an adequate motive for obedience and coincides with the realisation of freedom (James 1:25). It is the expression of the Truth, but this Truth is not finally presented in thoughts but in fact, not in abstract propositions but in a living Person.[7]

In this then lies the main idea of Christianity, that it presents the redemption, the perfection, the consummation of all finite being in union with God.[8]

Christianity is historical not simply or characteristically because Christ standing out before the world at a definite time and place proclaimed certain truths and laid down certain rules for the constitution and conduct of a society. It is historical because He offered Himself in His own Person, and He was shewn to be in the events of His Life, the revelation which He came to give.[9]

The divine revelation cannot be detached from the divine reality of the living Lord Jesus. The revelation of the gospel is the revelation of Himself. The "good news" is Jesus! The gospel revelation of God in Christ is not a differentiated philosophy with fragmented principles of belief and behavior. German martyr, Dietrich Bonhoeffer, wrote,

> "Christ is not a principle in accordance with which the whole world must be shaped. Christ is not the proclaimer of a system of what would be good today, here and at all times. Christ teaches no abstract ethics such as must at all costs be put into practice. Christ was not essentially a teacher and legislator, but a man, a real man like ourselves. It is not therefore His will that we should in our time be the adherents, exponents and advocates of a definite doctrine, but that we should be real men before God. ...What Christ does is precisely to give effect to reality. He is Himself the real man and consequently the foundation of all human reality."[10]

French author, Jacques Ellul, concurs,

> "There are no such things as 'Christian principles.' There is the Person of Christ, who is the principle of everything. If we wish to be faithful to Him, we cannot dream of reducing Christianity to a certain number of principles, the consequences of which can be logically deduced. This tendency to transform the work of the Living God into a philosophical doctrine is the constant temptation of theology, and their greatest disloyalty when they transform the action of the Spirit which brings forth fruit in themselves into an ethic, a new law, into 'principles' which only have to be 'applied.'"[11]

The divine work of God in Christ has been dualistically objectified and historically detached from the living person of the resurrected Lord. Based upon those historical and

238

theological objectivities of the restorative action of God in Christ, the spiritual work of God in Christ by the Spirit must be subjectively unified in the experience of men who are receptive to such in faith. Despite the tendency to shy away from such, due to mystic excesses and such ecclesiastical abuses as internal infusion and divinization that have arisen throughout the history of "Christian theology," there must be a balanced explanation and presentation of the objective and subjective, epistemological and experiential, historical and personal work of God in Christ. Apart from the experiential work of God in man, Christianity soon degenerates into merely static historical remembrances, theological categorizations, biblicist interpretations, moral conformations, liturgical repetitions, etc., as noted above. On the other hand, apart from the historical and theological foundations, Christianity easily degenerates into sensate subjectivism, emotive ecstaticism, ethereal mysticism, temporal existentialism, charismatic enthusiasm, etc. Thus the importance of our quest for a balanced Biblical understanding that integrates the external and internal by maintaining an integral unity of the eternal person and work of Jesus Christ.

In his book entitled *Christianity is Christ*, W.H. Griffith
Thomas concluded that,

> "The Christ of Experience cannot be sundered from the Christ
> of History, and the appeal to experience is impossible unless
> experience is based on historic fact. The history must guarantee the
> experience in the individual. ...If we lose our faith in the historic
> fact of the Christ of the Gospels it will not be long before we lose
> our faith in the experience of the Christ of today.[12]
> "...the central truth of Christianity (is) that the Holy Spirit
> brings to bear on our hearts and lives the presence and power of
> the living Christ, and thereby links together the Christ of History
> and the Christ of Faith. ...thus the work of the Holy Spirit in
> relation to Christ is the very heart of Christianity.[13]
> "Christ is essential, Christ is fundamental, Christ is all.[14]

Indeed, the intrinsic unity of the physically incarnated Jesus
and the resurrected, ascended Jesus poured out in the form
of the Spirit of Christ on Pentecost, continuing to function
in every age and unto eternity in the expression of His own
Being, must be maintained unequivocally as the essence of
Christianity.

As the particular purpose of this study is to call
Christian theology back to a personalized understanding of
the unified work of Christ in His ever-present spiritual
Being, we shall proceed to consider the divine reality of the
internalized presence and activity of the risen Lord Jesus by
His Spirit. In considering the subjective and experiential
implications of the life of Jesus Christ in Christians, we

must maintain the integral oneness of His Being and action by noting both the ontological essence of the indwelling Being of Jesus Christ in the Christian, as well as the dynamic expression of the functional activity of Jesus Christ in and through the Christian.

Ontological Essence of Jesus Christ in the Christian

The "bottom-line" reality of what it means to be a Christian is expressed by the apostle Paul in his epistle to the Romans, "If anyone does not have the Spirit of Christ, he is none of His" (Rom. 8:9), for "the Spirit Himself bears witness with our spirit that we are children of God" (Rom. 8:16). Apart from the indwelling presence and witness of the ontological essence of Christ by His Spirit, one is not a Christian and not participating in Christianity. "Christ in one" constitutes a "Christ-one," i.e. a Christian. This is the radical new reality that God made available in the new covenant, the essential presence of the very person, life and Being of the Spirit of Christ; the self-conveyance of Himself to the spirits of receptive humanity.

In this restoration of the Spirit of God to the spirits of men (cf. Gen. 2:7), so that men might function as God intended in His creative design, there is effected a spiritual

241

union whereby we become "one spirit" with Christ (I Cor. 6:17). This is not a psychological union whereby we keep Jesus in our thoughts and consciousness, nor is it a moral union whereby we are obliged to seek to conform to Jesus' example. Rather, it is a spiritual union whereby deity dwells and functions in man; Christ in the Christian. Jesus illustrated this spiritual condition to Nicodemus in the analogy of a "new birth," a spiritual regeneration whereby one is "born of the Spirit" (John 3:1-6).

It is extremely important to keep in mind that the presence of the risen Lord Jesus in the Christian is not to be divided from the person and presence of the Holy Spirit. The dissolution of the ontological essence of Jesus Christ from the Holy Spirit creates a defective Trinitarian perspective of God that has plagued "Christian theology" for centuries and remains a serious misrepresentation even in evangelical explanations. The Holy Spirit is not a substitute for Christ, nor is He a surrogate of Christ, but must be understood to be indissolubly one with Christ. Paul adequately reveals that the Spirit of God, the Spirit of Christ, and the Holy Spirit can be referred to inter-changably (Rom. 8:4-11) as the triune God, who is Spirit

(John 4:24), functions within the Christian. Swiss theologian, Karl Barth, noted that

> "the being and work of Jesus Christ in the form of the being and work of His Holy Spirit is the original and prefigurative existence of Christianity and Christians."[15]

The indwelling presence of the ontological essence of God the Father, Son and Holy Spirit in the spirit of a Christian constitutes the divine reality of a "new creature" in Christ. "If any man is in Christ, he is a new creature" (II Cor. 5:17). This is not an assumed identity wherewith to engage in role-playing of Christian living, but a new spiritual identity as a "new man" (Eph. 4:24; Col. 3:10) in Christ. The deepest sense of one's identity is in identification with the spiritual being that constitutes one's spiritual condition.

Here, again, we confront the dualistic detachment evident in Christian religion, that posits a separate and innate essence of human being with a self-generated capability to create or assume personal identity, nature, spirituality, character, image, life or immortality, independent of God. Only in spiritual union with the ontological essence of Jesus Christ can the Christian derive these spiritual realities, contingent upon and indivisible from Jesus Christ. Our spiritual nature as Christians is not an inherent human nature, but has been converted from a nature identified with wrath (Eph. 2:2) to "partaking of the divine nature" (II Peter 1:4) in unified coalition with the spiritual nature of God in Christ. We are not essentially spiritual, for that would be to deify man since only "God is Spirit" (John 4:24); but we derive our spirituality from spiritual connectivity either with the spirit of error or the spirit of truth (I John 4:6), the spirit of the world or the Spirit of God (I Cor. 2:12). Our character is not a conspicuous feature of personality in accord with social mores and values, but is determined by the essential impress of the character of the spirit that indwells us. The image of God in man is not comprised of innate features of human creatureliness, nor of disjoined reflections or representations of God in man, but the reality of the spiritual presence of God which allows for the visible expression of the character of God in our behavior when we have been spiritually renewed to such image in Jesus Christ (Col. 3:10). Even the essence of our personhood is not evaluated by the personality characteristics of mental, emotional and volitional function, but by our oneness with the Person of God in Christ who by His Trinitarian *homoousion* is the perfection of relational interaction in loving interpersonal relationships.

The entirety of who we are and what we do as Christians is derived from and contingent upon our spiritual union with the Spirit of Christ. This is not based upon an instrumental or causal connection with Christ whereby some "thing" other than Christ is extended to us, but is a personal and relational union whereby Christ Himself becomes the essence of all divine and spiritual realities in us.

"Christ is our life," explains the apostle Paul, for "our life is hidden with Christ in God" (Col. 3:3,4). Spiritual life is conveyed not by heritage or performance (John 1:13) or purchase, but through the figurative analogy of "new birth," being "born from above" (John 3:1-6) or "born of God" (John 1:13). The life that we receive in Christ is not separated apart from Jesus, nor is it a part of Jesus that can be partitively appropriated. Jesus is the spiritual life that we receive and participate in. "God has given us eternal life, and this life is in His Son" (I John 5:11). "I am...the life" (John 14:6), Jesus said, and "I came that you might have life" (John 10:10).

Concerning this eternal spiritual life, W. Ian Thomas explains,

> "Jesus Christ and eternal life are synonymous terms, and eternal life is none other than Jesus Christ Himself. ...If you have eternal life at all, it simply means that you have the Son, Jesus Christ..."
>
> "Eternal life is not a peculiar feeling inside! It is not your ultimate destination, to which you will go when you are dead. If you are born again, eternal life is that quality of life that you possess right now... He is that Life!"[16]

The spiritual life that we experience in Christ is the very resurrection-life of Jesus Christ. The historical event of Jesus' physical resurrection from the dead, allowed the risen and living Lord Jesus to invest His resurrection-life in all Christians by the Spirit. "I am the resurrection and the life" (John 11:25), Jesus explained. In explaining *The Mind of St. Paul*, William Barclay wrote,

> "To Paul the Resurrection was not a past fact, but a present power.
>
> "If Christ is risen from the dead, it means that it is possible for the Christian to live every moment of every day in the presence and the fellowship of the living Christ. It means that the Christian approaches no tasks alone, bears no sorrow alone, attacks no problem alone, faces no demand alone, endures no temptation alone. It means that Jesus Christ does not issue his commands, and then leave us to do our best to obey them alone, but that he is constantly with us to enable us to perform that which he commands.
>
> "To Paul the Resurrection of Jesus Christ was neither simply a fact in history nor a theological dogma. It was the supreme fact of

experience. It meant that all life is lived in the presence of the love and of the power of Jesus Christ."[17]

Lutheran professor, Karl Paul Donfried, comments similarly,

> "The early church did not ask its followers to simply imitate or observe some static principles of Christianity, but rather to so comprehend the significance of the Christ event that they could dynamically actualize its implications in the situation in which they lived. The freedom for this actualization and application to the concrete, existential situation can only be comprehended when one recognizes that these early Christians were not worshipping some dead prophet of Nazareth; rather, essential to their very existence was the conviction that this Jesus was raised from the dead by God, was now the Lord of the church, and present in its very life. It is this presence of the Risen One that both compelled and allowed the early church to engage in such vigorous and dynamic teaching and proclamation."[18]

The resurrection-life of the risen and living Lord Jesus is the ontological essence of Christianity. The continuum of His Life in a perpetuity that "cannot die" (John 11:26), allows His eternality to be expressed in immortality. Jesus "brought life and immortality to light through the gospel" (II Tim. 1:10). Such immortality of life is not inherent to man's humanity for "God alone possesses immortality" (I Tim. 6:16), nor is it a futuristic reward to be presented, but is inherent in the eternal resurrection-life of Jesus Christ. The Christian participates in and enjoys the perpetuity of eternal immortality only in spiritual union with the living Lord Jesus.

247

By these spiritual realities of the Christian's spiritual condition in regeneration we have sought to document the ontological essence of the indwelling Being of Jesus Christ in the Christian. "Do you not recognize this about yourselves, that Jesus Christ is in you?" (II Cor. 13:5), Paul queried the Corinthians. To the Colossians, he explained that the spiritual mystery of the gospel is "Christ in you, the hope of glory" (Col. 1:27).

Dynamic Expression of Jesus Christ through the Christian

To keep the divine Being and activity integrated and unified, we proceed to consider the dynamic expression of the functional activity of Jesus Christ in and through Christian behavior. The spiritual condition of the Christian, constituted by the indwelling presence of His life, allows for the self-expression of His Being in Christian behavior. The essence and expression of Christ's life are conjoined by Paul when he wrote to the Galatians, "it is no longer I who live, but Christ lives in me; and the life that I now live in the flesh I live by faith in the Son of God who loved me and gave Himself for me" (Gal. 2:20).

The life of Jesus Christ within the spirit of the Christian is not just a deposit to guarantee future heavenly benefits.

Such a static and detached understanding of the Christian life encourages Christians to "hold on," wait, and endure the pathos of the present, because the past is forgiven and the future is assured. It misreads the gospel as a heavenly fire-insurance policy for the avoidance of hell. The objective of participating in Christianity and the Christian life is not just to avoid hell and get passage to heaven, but to allow the dynamic expression of the life of Jesus Christ by His Spirit to function in human behavior to the glory of God on the way to heaven (if such is to be perceived merely as locative and future). Regeneration of spiritual condition is but a crisis with a view to a living process!

Christian living is not generated, produced or manufactured by the Christian in response to, or appreciation of, Christ's redemptive work or spiritual presence. Jesus' physical behavior and ministry on earth was not generated by His own initiative (John 8:28; 12:49), but by the divine presence of the Father abiding in Him and doing His works (John 14:10), and likewise the Christian life is not self-generated by the initiative of the Christian, but is enacted by the dynamic expression of the life of Jesus Christ through the Christian. Thomas Merton explained that "Jesus creates it (the Christian life) in our

249

souls by the action of His Spirit."[19] The dynamic of God's grace in Jesus Christ is the impetus of the Christian life.

As previously noted, Christianity is not morality. The Christian life is not human and religious attempts to implement a theory for living a good and moral life by conformity to behavioral rules and regulations. It is not even the attempt to put into practice the moral teachings of Jesus. Rather, the indwelling Christ-life is to be dynamically expressed in the behavior of a Christian. C.S. Lewis explains,

> "the Christian thinks any good he does comes from the Christ-life inside him. He does not think God will love us because we are good, but that God will make us good because He loves us."
> "...when Christians say the Christ-life is in them, they do not mean simply something mental or moral. When they speak of being 'in Christ' or of Christ being 'in them,' this is not simply a way of saying that they are thinking about Christ or copying Him. They mean that Christ is actually operating through them..."[20]
> "(the) Christian idea of 'putting on Christ'... It is the whole of Christianity. Christianity offers nothing else at all. It differs from ordinary ideas of 'morality' and 'being good.'"[21]

Neither is the Christian life an attempt to follow Jesus' example and "imitate His virtues."[22] Contrary to the classic inculcations to the *Imitation of Christ* (Thomas a Kempis) by walking *In His Steps* (Charles Sheldon) in order to be *Like Christ* (Andrew Murray), the Christian life is not an attempt at duplication. Methodist pastor, Maxie Dunnam, explained that,

"...to see the patterning of lives after Jesus as the essence of Christianity misses the point. This has been the major failure of the Christian Church since the second century on. To emphasize following Jesus as the heart of Christianity is to reduce it to a religion of morals and ethics and denude it of power. This has happened over and over again in Christian history—the diminishing of the role of Jesus to merely an example for us to follow."[23]

Ortiz admonishes Christians to,

"Stop trying to copy the Jesus of nearly 2000 years ago, and let the living Christ flow through your character. You are an expression of the glorified, eternal Christ who lives within you."[24]

The Christian life is not an imitation of Jesus' life, but the manifestation of His life and Being in our behavior. The Apostle Paul was desirous that "the life of Jesus should be manifested in our mortal bodies" (II Cor. 4:10,11).

Explaining to His disciples their inability to reproduce the Christian life, Jesus indicated, "Apart from Me, you can do nothing" (John 15:5). There is nothing that a Christian can originate or activate that constitutes or demonstrates Christianity, that qualifies as Christian behavior, or that glorifies God. "I am the vine, you are the branches" (John 15:5) was the analogy that Jesus utilized to illustrate the necessity of allowing His life sustenance to flow through the Christian's bodily behavior, whereby the Christian might bear (not produce) the fruit of His character. The character of Christ lived out in Christians is the "fruit of the Spirit, which is love, joy, peace, patience, kindness, goodness, faithfulness, gentleness, and self-control" (Gal. 5:22,23).

The fruit of Christ's character is also the "fruit of righteousness" (Phil. 1:11; James 3:18). The divine character of righteousness (I John 2:29; 3:7) personified in "the Righteous One" (Acts 3:13; 7:52; 22:14;I John 2:1), Jesus Christ, allows the Christian to "become righteous" (II Cor. 5:21) and "be made righteous" (Rom. 5:19), as "Christ becomes to us...righteousness" (I Cor. 1:30). The understanding of righteousness must not be objectified only in "positional truths" of declaration, imputation, reckoning and reconciliation, with no practical implication of our bodily members being "instruments of righteousness" (Rom. 6:13) in the conveyance of Christ's character.

"Having been reconciled, we shall be saved by His life" (Rom. 5:10), Paul explains. Christians live by "the saving life of Christ."[25] That is why Paul could also say, "for me to live is Christ" (Phil. 1:21). Salvation is not simply a static event of regenerative conversion, but is the dynamic expression of Christ's life that causes us to be "made safe" from misuse and dysfunction, in order to function as God intended by His presence and activity in us.

All of the deeds or works of Christian living are but the outworking of Christ's activity. "We are His workmanship, created in Christ Jesus for good works, which He has prepared beforehand that we should walk in them" (Eph. 2:10). We allow for the outworking of Christ's work by recognizing that "God is at work in us, both to will and to work for His good pleasure" (Phil. 2:12,13). To claim Christian faith without any of the consequent outworking of Christ's character and activity, is to evidence the invalidity of such faith (*cf.* James 2:14,17,26).

Christian ministry is likewise, not something that the Christian does to serve Jesus. "God is not served with human hands, as though He needed anything" (Acts 17:25). Rather, we recognize that the "same God works all things in all Christians" (I Cor. 12:6). Together with Paul we affirm that "we are not adequate to consider anything as coming from ourselves, but our adequacy is of God" (II Cor. 3:5). This is why Paul declared, "I will not presume to speak of anything except what Christ has accomplished through me" (Rom. 15:18).

God in Christ by His Spirit empowers, enables, energizes and enacts all Christian behavior and ministry as the dynamic expression of the life of Jesus Christ. Christianity is Christ. Christian living is the life and character of Jesus Christ lived out through the Christian.

Some would object that this thesis is a form of divine determinism that impinges upon man's freedom of choice, but such is not valid for man is definitely responsible to exercise the choice of faith that allows for the receptivity of God's activity in him, both initially and continually. Others would object that attributing all Christian activity to Christ encourages passivism and acquiescence, but notice the words of Paul, "I labor, striving according to His power, which mightily works within me" (Col. 1:29). God is an active God, always acting out of His Being and character, and those available to Him will inevitably be involved in active expressions of the Christ-life.

Continuing then, the entirety of this divine, spiritual reality of Christ's presence and function as Christianity, must be understood not only individually in the life of each Christian (as we have been doing), but also collectively or corporately in the whole of the Church of Jesus Christ.

The ontological essence of Jesus Christ collectively embodied in all Christians comprises the Body of Christ, the Church (Eph. 1:22,23; Col. 1:18,24). Not only is Christ in us individually, but He is "in us" collectively (*cf.* I Cor. 3:16), and we are "in Him" together (cf. Eph. 1:13). "We are all one in Christ Jesus" (Gal. 3:28), irrespective of race, gender, age, nationality, education, intelligence, personality patterns, doctrinal opinions, or denominational preferences. Dietrich Bonhoeffer expressed the singular essence of the Body "in Christ" in these words:

> "The Church is the real presence of Christ. Once we have realized this truth we are well on the way to recovering an aspect of the Church's being which has been sadly neglected in the past. We should think of the Church not as an institution, but as a person, though of course a person in a unique sense.[26]
>
> "Through his Spirit, the crucified and risen Lord exists as the Church, as the new man. It is just as true to say that this Body is the new humanity as to say that he is God incarnate dwelling in eternity.[27]
>
> "The Church of Christ is the presence of Christ through the Holy Spirit. In this way the life of the Body of Christ becomes our own life. In Christ we no longer live our own lives, but he lives His life in us. The life of the faithful in the Church is indeed the life of Christ in them."[28]

Swiss author, Manfred Haller, also sees the singular unity of Christ and the Church.

> "Christ is the essence and nature of the church by the Holy Spirit. He is her content, her structure, her fullness, and she is for her part Christ's fullness."[29]

255

"In modern parlance, church is an institution, a form of Christian community, a set of people believing in Christ (or at least having some concept of God) which convenes regularly. When we talk about church, we immediately picture a number of people who, on the basis of some common understanding or arrangement, have formed a Christian association. ...When Paul thought of the church, however, he thought of Christ. The idea that the church could be anything beyond the embodiment of Christ never crossed his mind."[30]

"Christ and the church are one single reality! The body is not an attachment to Christ; it embodies Him. It gives expression to Christ – the whole Christ – and it carries Him within it. In the church, in the body, Christ Himself lives and acts and speaks. The church is the corporate Christ – Christ in the saints through the Holy Spirit. This indwelling Christ is her nature and structure, her unity, truth and certainty; He is everything to her. And Christ is in every member!"[31]

"Christ and the church are absolutely and indivisibly one. The church is utterly absorbed in the experience of the risen and present Lord. The inner reality and presence of Christ stamps her indelibly. She is directed by Him and held together by Him, and the very length and breadth of her is the person of Christ Jesus. Her authority is His, her mind is His mind, and her holiness His holiness. She has nothing of her own."[32]

"The church has only this task: to embody Christ, manifest His nature, demonstrate God's love to the world and proclaim His Lordship over all things."[33]

As the ontological essence of the Church, the living Lord Jesus is also the dynamic expression of all that transpires in the Church – His Body. Jesus Christ in each individual Christian relates to Himself in another Christian, allowing for interactive interpersonal relationships that comprise a loving social community. Early observers of the Church, of Christianity, marveled at how the Christians "loved one another." In the expression of Christ's character

256

of love, they ministered together in the spiritual giftedness of Christ's functional service to one another, as was the intent of the Church's functionality.

Jesus promised that the Church, thus functioning by the presence and activity of His life, would overcome all odds. "Upon this rock I will build My church; and the gates of Hades shall not overpower it" (Matt. 16:18). B.F. Westcott observed that "the history of the Christian Church is the history of the victories of the Risen Christ gained through the Spirit sent in His name."[34] "We see a Divine Life manifested...from age to age through a Divine society."[35] The conclusion of James Denny was that, "without Christ there would be no Church and no ministry at all; everything we call Christian is absolutely dependent on Him."[36]

Have we not sufficiently documented that Jesus Christ is the singular essence and expression of the gospel, of the revelation of God, of Christianity, of the Church? Everything "Christian" is derived from the Being and activity of Jesus. All of Christianity is contingent and dependent on Him, and expressive of Him. Christianity is Christ!

When Jesus announced to His disciples, "I am the way, the truth, and the life" (John 14:6), He was declaring that all was inherent in Him. He is the modality, reality and vitality of God, and thus of Christianity and the Church. He does not just teach us the way of God or guide us to the divine way, but His very Being is the way of God's self-revelation to man, the modality of spiritual union with God and proper human function. He does not simply teach truth propositions about God apart from Himself, but His very Being is the self-authenticating Truth of God, the reality of Christianity. He does not offer us an historical example of life or a commodity of "eternal life," but His very Being is the self-expression of the living God, the dynamic vitality of Christian life. He could just as well have said, "I am Christianity!"

Disintegration of the Gospel

How important is this integration of Christ's person and work, the integral oneness of His being and action? Is it really of serious import to insist that the unity of His essence and expression be maintained? Should we endeavor to challenge the traditional dualistic detachments of "Christian religion," and upset the religious status-quo that separates Christ from that activity that goes by His name?

This author believes that it is imperative that we address the issue of the detachment and disjuncture of Christianity from Christ, for such a perversion constitutes a disintegration of the gospel, the revelation of God in Christ. The issue at hand is but another form of that initially addressed by Paul in his epistle to the Galatians, when he confronted the Galatian believers who were being duped into denying that Christianity was constituted in the life of Christ alone without any encumbrances of additional belief or action. Paul accused those who succumbed to such disconnected accretions of a circumscribed ritual, of "deserting Christ, who called them by His grace, for another gospel which is not good news at all, but a distortion worthy only of damnation" (Gal. 1:6-9).

If the *homoousion* issue of the integral oneness of the Trinity was important enough to address at the Council of Nicea in the fourth century. If *the sola gratia, sola fide, sola scriptura, sola Christus* issue of the singularity of the redemptive efficacy of Christ's justifying and sanctifying work received by faith was important enough to address in the Reformation of the sixteenth century. Then, the issue of the integral oneness of the ontological essence and dynamic expression of Jesus Christ in Christianity and the Church is certainly timely and important enough to address in the twenty-first century.

The disintegration of Christ and Christianity in contemporary "Christian religion" allows the ontological essence of Jesus Christ in the Christian individual to degenerate into an obliging endorsement of history or theology. The dynamic expression of Jesus Christ in the Christian individual is diminished to the dictated exercise and effort of moralism and ethics. The ontological essence of Jesus Christ in the Church collectively is reduced to an organizational entity of ecclesiasticism. The dynamic expression of Jesus Christ in His Body is replaced with the determined enterprise of religious planning and programs. Christianity is thus mutilated and mutated by man-made "Christian religion" which has no value before God (cf. Col. 2:23).

Consider the serious logical consequences of allowing Christianity and Christ to be thus divided, divorced, and disintegrated. Without the recognition of the ontological and dynamic connection and union of Christ and Christianity, there is an inevitable deficient and defective understanding of the Trinity, of God's action in the Christian and the Church through the Son, by the Holy

Spirit. When Jesus Christ, the Righteous One (Acts 3:14; 7:52) is separated and severed from the dynamic expression of Christian righteousness, with the subsequent insistence on pious performance of Christian living, then the efficacy of the death of Christ is denied and the cross is but a redundant, superfluous and unnecessary tragedy of history (*cf.* Gal. 2:21). When "Christian religion" mutates Christianity into mere morality generated by the self-effort of human ability, then "the stumbling block of the cross has been abolished" (Gal. 5:11), as the "finished work" of Christ (John 19:30) is left unfinished, to be completed by human commitment and ability. When Christianity is conceived of as anything less that the ontological presence and dynamic activity of the living Lord Jesus, then some separated and detached entity is formed and formulated, whether it be in thought construction or ecclesiastical construction, and such construct becomes the object of idolatry. These are serious abdications and aberrations that must be addressed and challenged.

Though some have called for a "new reformation,"[37] such could merely imply a re-forming of the existent theological belief-systems or ecclesiastical constructions, which would be inadequate. What we need is a complete restoration of the recognition of the reality of the risen Lord Jesus as the essence and expression of Christianity, which constitutes the restoration of humanity to God's functional intent by the indwelling function of Jesus Christ in the Christian.

The affirmation that Christianity is Christ, that "Christianity is the divine,"[38] is not merely advocacy of another variant epistemological ideology or the defense of a more precise orthodox belief-system. This is a call to return to the reality of the risen and living Lord Jesus Christ as the ontological essence and behavioral expression of Christianity. There will, without a doubt, be some theological objectivists who will attempt to pass off this integral Christocentric emphasis as perfectionist idealism or subjective mysticism. They will insist on the retention of detached cerebral and ecclesiastical objectivities that deny and disallow the real and vital spiritual experience of the living Spirit of Christ, for themselves and for others.

John R.W. Stott vividly portrays pictures in words when he writes that "Christianity without Christ is a chest without a treasure, a frame without a portrait, a corpse without breath."[39] Are we content to sit idly by and allow "Christian religion" and its empty, sterile theology

262

misrepresent Christianity in such a lifeless and fallacious manner? Now is the time to unashamedly affirm that "Christianity is Christ," and to witness such personally by allowing the resurrection-life of the living Lord Jesus to be "manifested in our mortal bodies" (II Cor. 4:10,11) by the grace of God unto the glory of God.

ENDNOTES

Chapter One – Christianity is not religion

1   Luther, Martin, source unknown.
2   Kierkegaard, Soren, *Attack on Christendom*. Princeton: Princeton Univ. Press. 1968.
3   Bonhoeffer, Dietrich, *Letters and Papers from Prison*..
4   Barth, Karl, *Church Dogmatics*. Vol. I, Pt. 2. Edinburgh: T&T Clark. 1956. pg. 280.
5   *Ibid*., pg 294.
6   *Ibid*., pg. 298.
7   *Ibid*., pg. 299.
8   *Ibid*., pg. 302.
9   *Ibid*., pg. 303.
10 *Ibid*., pg. 308.
11 *Ibid*., pg. 325.
12 Ellul, Jacques, *Living Faith: Belief and Doubt in a Perilous World*. San Francisco: Harper and Row.1983. pg. 123.
13 *Ibid*., pg. 129.
14 *Ibid*., pg. 137.
15 Capon, Robert, *Between Noon and Three: A Parable of Romance, Law, and the Outrage of Grace*. San Francisco: Harper and Row. 1982. pg. 136.
16 *Ibid*., pg. 166.
17 *Ibid*., pg. 167.
18 Marchant, JRV and Charles, JF, (eds), *Cassell's Latin Dictionary*. London: Cassell and Co. pg. 478.
19 Ayto, John, *Dictionary of Word Origins*. New York: Arcade Pub., 1990. pg. 438.
20 Jones, E. Stanley, *The Christ of the Indian Road*. New York: Grosset and Dunlap. 1925. pgs. 53,54.
21 Bloom, Harold, *The American Religion*.
22 The French word for "Christianity" is "*Christianisme*"
23 Nolan, Albert, *Jesus Before Christianity*. Maryknoll: Orbis Books, 1976. pg. 3.

24   Fowler, James A., *Jesus Confronts Religion: A Commentary on the Four Gospel-records in Harmony.* Fallbrook: C.I.Y. Publishing, 1996.

25   Fowler, James A., *Jesus Christ: Victor Over Religion; A Commentary on Revelation.* Fallbrook: C.I.Y. Publishing, 1994.

26   Pascal, Blaise, *Provincial Letters.* In The Great Books of the Western World. Vol. 33, Chicago: Encyclopedia Britannica, Inc., 1952.

27   Thomas, W. Ian, *The Mystery of Godliness.* Grand Rapids: Zondervan Pub. 1964. pg. 42.

28   Lewis, C.S., *The Screwtape Letters.* New York: Macmillan Co., 1959.

29   Lewis, C.S., *The World's Last Night and Other Essays.* "Screwtape Proposes a Toast." New York: Harcourt, Brace Jovanovich, 1960. pg. 70.

30   Pascal, Blaise, as quoted by Charles Colson in *Kingdoms in Conflict.* Grand Rapids: Zondervan Pub. Co. 1987. pg.43.

31   Olson, Norman, "Good News Broadcaster" magazine, July/Aug 1982. pgs. 36,37.

32   Hunt, Dave, *"The Berean Call"* newsletter. October 1993.

33   James, William, *Varieties of Religious Experience.*

Chapter Two – Christianity is not Book-religion

1   Urban, James R., "The Bible Man's Only Hope", published by Mission to Catholics International, Inc., San Diego, CA, n.d.

2   Urban, James R., *Ibid.*

3   Urban, James R., *Ibid.*

4   Urban, James R., *Ibid.*

5   MacArthur, John, Jr., *Our Sufficiency in Christ,* Dallas: Word Publishing, 1991, pg. 87.

6   MacArthur, John, Jr., *Ibid.,* pg. 87.

7   MacArthur, John, Jr., *Ibid.,* pg. 90.

8   MacArthur, John, Jr., *Ibid.,* pg. 165.

9   MacArthur, John, Jr., *Ibid.,* pg. 99.

10   MacArthur, John, Jr., *Ibid.,* pg. 111.

11   MacArthur, John, Jr., *Ibid.,* pg. 165.

12   MacArthur, John, Jr., *Ibid.,* pg. 144.

13   MacArthur, John, Jr., *Ibid.,* pg. 146.

14   MacArthur, John, Jr., *Ibid.,* pg. 163.
15   MacArthur, John, Jr., *Ibid.,* pg. 162.
16   MacArthur, John, Jr., *Ibid.,* pg. 164.
17   MacArthur, John, Jr., *Ibid.,* pg. 165.
18   MacArthur, John, Jr., *Ibid.,* pg. 164.
19   MacArthur, John, Jr., *Ibid.,* pg. 163.
20   Lightner, Robert P., "The Written Word and the Living Word" in the *Fundamentalist Journal,* May 1983, reprinted from his book *The God of the Bible,* Baker Book House, 1978.
21   Lightner, Robert P., *Ibid.*
22   Lightner, Robert P., *Ibid.*
23   Lightner, Robert P., *Ibid.*
24   Lightner, Robert P., *Ibid.*
25   Lightner, Robert P., *Ibid.*
26   Lightner, Robert P., *Ibid.*
27   Lightner, Robert P., *Ibid.*
28   Lightner, Robert P., *Ibid.*
29   Lightner, Robert P., *Ibid.*
30   Brinsmead, Robert, "Word of God in the New Testament", *Verdict,* No. 15.

Chapter Three – Christianity is not Morality

1   Ellul, Jacques, *To Will and To Do.* Philadelphia: Pilgrim Pr. 1969. pg. 201.
2   Ellul, Jacques, *The Subversion of Christianity.* Grand Rapids: Eerdmans Pub. 1986. pg. 69.
3   Lewis, C.S., *Mere Christianity.* New York: Macmillan Pub. 1952. pg. 130.
4   Ellul, Jacques, *To Will and To Do.* pg. 30.
5   Thomas, W. Ian, *The Mystery of Godliness.* Grand Rapids: Zondervan. 1964. pg. 50.
6   Lewis, C.S., *Mere Christianity.* pg. 130.
7   Stewart, James S., *A Man in Christ.* New York: Harper & Brothers. n.d., pg. 168.
8   Lake, Frank, *Clinical Theology.* New York: Crossroad. 1986. pg. 168.
9   Ellul, Jacques, *The Ethics of Freedom.* Grand Rapids: Eerdmans. 1976. pg. 239.
10   Thomas, W. Ian, *The Mystery of Godliness.* pg. 43.

11   Ellul, Jacques, *To Will and To Do*. pg. 71.
12   Ellul, Jacques, *To Will and To Do*. pg. 224.
13   Ellul, Jacques, *To Will and To Do*. pg. 224.
14   Lewis, C.S., *Mere Christianity*. pg. 166.
15   Lewis, C.S., *Mere Christianity*. pg. 64.
16   Ellul, Jacques, *To Will and To Do*. pg. 210.
17   Ellul, Jacques, *To Will and To Do*. pg. 34.
18   Lewis, C.S., *Mere Christianity*. pg. 130.
19   Ellul, Jacques, *To Will and To Do*. pg. 41.
20   Torrance, Thomas F., *The Doctrine of Grace in the Apostolic Fathers*. Edinburgh: Oliver and Boyd. 1948. pg. 139.
21   Ellul, Jacques, *The Subversion of Christianity*. pg. 89.

Chapter Four – Christianity is not a Belief-system

1   Torrance, T.F., *Karl Barth, Biblical and Evangelical Theologian,* page 215, Edinburgh: T & T Clark, 1990
2   Torrance, T.F., *Ibid.* page 122.
3   Edwards, Gene, *Church Unity...How to Get There*, page 99, Auburn: Christian Books Publishing House, 1991.
4   Stewart, James S., *A Man in Christ,* New York: Harper and Brothers.

Chapter Five – Christianity is not Epistemology

1   Torrance, Thomas F., *Karl Barth, Biblical and Evangelical Theologian*. Edinburgh: T&T Clark, 1990. pg. 215.
2   Bock, Darrell L., *Bibliotheca Sacra,* "A Review of 'The Gospel According to Jesus'", Jan.-Mar., 1989. pg. 38.
3   Bock, *Ibid.* pg. 38
4   Bock, *Ibid.* pg. 32
5   Hodges, Zane, *The Gospel Under Siege, A Study on Faith and Works*. Dallas: Redencion Viva, 1981.
6   MacArthur, John F. Jr., *The Gospel According to Jesus*. Grand Rapids: Zondervan. 1988.
7   Bock, Darrel L., *Bibliotheca Sacra,* Review... pg. 21.
8   Bock, *Ibid.* pg. 22.
9   Hunt, Dave, *The Berean Call*. April, 1993. pg. 1.
10 Hunt, *Ibid.* pg. 1.

11 Hunt, *Ibid.* pg. 1.
12 Robbins, John W., *The Trinity Review.* April, 1993. pg. 4.
13 Robbins, *Ibid.* pg. 4.
14 MacArthur, John F. Jr., *The Gospel According to Jesus.*
15 Kittel, Gerhard (ed*.), Theological Dictionary of the New Testament.* Vol. II. "*euangellion*", pg. 733.
16 Kittel, *Ibid.* pg. 734.
17 Bock, Darrell, *Bibliotheca Sacra*, Review... pg. 32.
18 Bock, Darrell, *Bibliotheca Sacra.* Apr.-June 1986.

Chapter Six – Christianity is not Role-playing

1 Shakespeare, William, *As You Like It, Act 2, Scene 6. The Plays and Sonnets of William Shakespeare. Vol. I. Great Books of the Western World.* Chicago: Encyclopedia Britannica Inc. 1952. pg. 608.
2 Maugham, W. Somerset, *The Summing Up.* 1938. pg. 39.
3 Calvin, John, *Commentary upon the Acts of the Apostles. Vol. I.* Grand Rapids: Baker Book House, pg. 559.

Chapter Seven – Christianity is not an ...ism

1 Kierkegaard, Soren, *Attack on Christendom.* Princeton: Princeton University Press. 1944. pg. 160.
2 *Ibid.*, pgs. 162,163.
3 Ellul, Jacques, *The Subversion of Christianity.* Grand Rapids: William B. Eerdmans Pub. Co., 1986.
4 *Ibid.*, pgs. 10,11.

Chapter Eight – Christianity is not Problem-solving

1 Ellul, Jacques, *The Ethics of Freedom.* Grand Rapids: Wm. B. Eerdmans Publishing Co., 1976. pg. 373.
2 Thomas, W. Ian, *The Mystery of Godliness.* Grand Rapids: Zondervan Publishing House. 1972. pg. 17.
3 Capon, Robert Farrar, *The Mystery of Christ.* Grand Rapids: Wm. B. Eerdmans Pub. Co., 1993. pg. 62.

4 Ellul, Jacques, *The False Presence of the Kingdom*. New York: Seabury Press. 1972. pg. 125.
5 Ogilvie, Lloyd, *If God Cares, Why Do I Still Have Problems?* Minneapolis: Grason, 1985.
6 Hansel, Tim, *Eating Problems for Breakfast: A Simple, Creative Approach to Solving Any Problem*. Dallas: Word Publishing, 1988. pg. 17
7 Ellul, Jacques, *op. cit., Ethics of Freedom*. pg. 475.
8 Fowler, James A., *The Uselessness of Usefulness and the Usefulness of Uselessness*. Fallbrook: C.I.Y. Publishing. 1996.
9 Ellul, Jacques, *The Presence of the Kingdom*. Philadelphia: Westminster Press. 1951. pgs. 91-93.
10 Ellul, Jacques, *op. cit., Ethics of Freedom*. pg. 300.

Chapter Ten – Christianity is Christ

1 Lewis, C.S., *Mere Christianity: What One Must Believe to Be a Christian*. New York: Macmillan Publishing Co. 1978. pg. 62.
2 Nevin, John W., *The Mystical Presence*. Philadelphia: United Church Press. 1846. pg. 216.
3 Torrance, Thomas F., *Reality and Evangelical Theology*. Philadelphia: Westminster Press. 1982. pg. 16.
4 *Ibid.*, pg. 18.
5 Barclay, William. *The Mind of St. Paul*. London: Fontana Books. 1965. pg. 87.
6 Ortiz, Juan Carlos, *Living With Jesus Today*. London: Triangle Books. 1984. pgs. 18,19.
7 Westcott, Brooke Foss, *The Gospel of Life: Thoughts Introductory to the Study of Christian Doctrine*. London: Macmillan and Co.1895. pg. 249.
8 *Ibid.* pg. 250.
9 *Ibid.* pg. 255.
10 Bonhoeffer, Dietrich, *Ethics*. New York: Macmillan Publishing Co. 1976. pg. 22.
11 Ellul, Jacques, *The Presence of the Kingdom*. Philadelphia: Westminster Press. 1951. pg. 52.
12 Thomas, W.H. Griffith, *Christianity is Christ*. London: Longmans, Green and Co. 1916. pg. 115.
13 *Ibid.* pg. 117.

14 *Ibid.* pg. 118.
15 Barth, Karl, *Church Dogmatics.* Vol. IV, Part I, "The Doctrine of Reconciliation." Edinburgh: T&T Clark, 1988. pg. 149.
16 Thomas, Maj. W. Ian, *The Saving Life of Christ.* Grand Rapids: Zondervan Publishing Co. 1961. pg. 149.
17 Barclay, William. *op. cit.,* pg. 89.
18 Donfried, Karl Paul, *The Dynamic Word: New Testament Insights for Contemporary Christians.* San Francisco: Harper and Row. 1981. pg. 3.
19 Merton, Thomas, *The New Man.* New York: The Noonday Press. 1961. pg. 165.
20 Lewis, C.S., *op. cit.* pg. 64.
21 *Ibid.,* pg. 166.
22 Merton, Thomas, *op. cit.,* pg. 169.
23 Dunnam, Maxie, *Alive in Christ: The Dynamic Process of Spiritual Formation.* Nashville: Abingdon Press. 1982. pgs. 110,111.
24 Ortiz, Juan Carlos, op. cit., pg. 42.
25 Thomas, Maj. W. Ian, *op. cit.* Title of book.
26 Bonhoeffer, Dietrich, *The Cost of Discipleship.* New York: Macmillan Publishing Co. pg. 269.
27 *Ibid.,* pg. 271.
28 *Ibid.,* pg. 272.
29 Haller, Manfred, *Christ as All in All.* Sargent: The SeedSowers. 1996. pg. 105.
30 *Ibid.,* pg. 116.
31 *Ibid.,* pg. 118.
32 *Ibid.,* pg. 121.
33 *Ibid.,* pg. 156.
34 Westcott, B.F., *op. cit.* pg. 278.
35 *Ibid.,* pg. 281.
36 Denney, James, *Jesus and the Gospels: Christianity Justified in the Mind of Christ.* London: Hodder and Stoughton. 1908. pg. 27.
37 Torrance, Thomas F., *Theology in Reconstruction.* Grand Rapids: William B. Eerdmans. 1965. pgs. 259-283.
38 Kierkegaard, Soren, *Attack on Christendom.* Princeton: Princeton University Press. 1968. pgs. 102, 132.
39 Stott, John R.W., *Focus on Christ.* New York: Collins. 1979. pg. 155.